SpringerBriefs in Economics

SpringerBriefs present concise summaries of cutting-edge research and practical applications across a wide spectrum of fields. Featuring compact volumes of 50 to 125 pages, the series covers a range of content from professional to academic. Typical topics might include:

- A timely report of state-of-the art analytical techniques
- A bridge between new research results, as published in journal articles, and a contextual literature review
- A snapshot of a hot or emerging topic
- An in-depth case study or clinical example
- A presentation of core concepts that students must understand in order to make independent contributions

SpringerBriefs in Economics showcase emerging theory, empirical research, and practical application in microeconomics, macroeconomics, economic policy, public finance, econometrics, regional science, and related fields, from a global author community.

Briefs are characterized by fast, global electronic dissemination, standard publishing contracts, standardized manuscript preparation and formatting guidelines, and expedited production schedules.

Tomasz Żylicz

Marketable Permits

Springer

Tomasz Żylicz
University of Warsaw
Warsaw, Poland

ISSN 2191-5504 ISSN 2191-5512 (electronic)
SpringerBriefs in Economics
ISBN 978-3-032-12132-5 ISBN 978-3-032-12133-2 (eBook)
https://doi.org/10.1007/978-3-032-12133-2

This Springer imprint is published by the registered company Springer Nature Switzerland AG
The registered company address is: Gewerbestrasse 11, 6330 Cham, Switzerland

Acknowledgements I am grateful to my professional colleagues and students for our endless discussions about the merits and traps of marketable permits. Ms. Lorrain Klimowich of Springer invited reviewers of the earlier draft, requested revisions, and helped me to navigate through the complex editorial procedure. I thought that my language was perfect and my exposition was clear. However, my daughter Marta **Ż**ylicz demonstrated that I was wrong and suggested many improvements. I trust that readers who would like to go beyond a standard environmental economics text will find my book useful.

Competing Interests The author has no competing interests to declare that are relevant to the content of this manuscript.

Contents

Chapter 1
Introduction

Marketable permits—also called tradable permits or transferable permits—differ from non-marketable ones in that they need not necessarily be used strictly for the purpose that they were granted; some scholars refer to 'tradable entitlement systems'. If a firm does not use them fully, the unused part can be stored for the future or used by another firm. And vice versa: if a firm wishes to do more than its permit allows, the missing part can be purchased. Transfers may involve different entities. Some systems also allow transactions within a single firm; the unused permits can be used by the same firm in the future. Alternatively, a firm can deprive itself of a future use by using the permit earlier than it was originally granted for.

Tradable permits to pollute are the best known but the instrument can regulate whatever needs to be regulated. Hence we have harvest quotas when fishermen do not catch the exact amount that they are allowed to. Similarly, there are transferable development rights if—as a result of local spatial management regulations—developers are unable to do something that can be done elsewhere. Finally, there are commitments to comply with certain requirements where not individual but aggregate outcomes count. Here, too, firms can transfer their individual accomplishments.

Marketable permits allow to achieve a given objective at the least cost: if something can be done cheaper than where the permit turned out to be insufficient, the firm that holds this insufficient permit finds it attractive to buy the missing part elsewhere. And conversely, if a firm sees that it can achieve something cheaper than elsewhere, it does not use its permit fully and sells the unused part. As a result of their tradability, permits go where they are needed most. The cost saving is especially high when agents who are regulated through marketable permits face large differences in compliance efforts.

Theoretically, the same result could be achieved by giving more permits to firms that need them most, and less to firms that can do the same thing easier. To this end, administrators who issue permits should make decisions based on the costs implied by depriving a firm of a permit. In reality, however, administrators do not have

T. Żylicz, *Marketable Permits*, SpringerBriefs in Economics,
https://doi.org/10.1007/978-3-032-12133-2_1

such information. Hence permits result not so much from the costs but rather from persuading administrators to give a generous allocation (possibly by cheating them). Firms often blackmail their administrators and threaten them with the perspective of a shutdown, firing workers, losing to foreign competitors, etc. For the sake of peace and quiet, administrators sometimes allocate non-marketable permits that are excessive—given the firms' actual situation—and environmentally harmful (in the first place).

The marketability of permits frees administrators from such pressure and triggers firms' creativity in achieving sectorial or regional objectives—determined by the sum of permits—at the least cost. Administrators are not afraid of being blackmailed and can focus on what they should, i.e. on using the permits to protect the environment.

Marketable permits are no longer a novelty or an experiment; they are an indispensable environmental policy instrument. While early environmental economics textbooks typically covered them in a short chapter (see e.g. (Baumol and Oates 1988)), marketable permits have been given more attention lately (see e.g. (Phaneuf and Requate 2016), (Lewis and Tietenberg 2019), or (Buchholz et al. 2024)). Nevertheless, they have never received a systematic exposition that would address both the theoretical foundations and policy relevance. This text aims to provide students with basic knowledge of the merits and policy applications of marketable permits. Implementations of these are numerous. In many cases, however, it is not actually clear whether the policies applied do in fact have the attributes of the instrument; permits are sometimes called 'marketable', but upon closer scrutiny it turns out that they are not. The examples given in Chaps. 6–7 and 9–10 refer to applications that should be considered marketable permits beyond any doubt.

In some books (e.g. Hanley et al. 2007), marketable permits are considered jointly with Pigouvian taxes as applications of economic incentives. Although both instruments share common characteristics (see Sect. 2.3), they belong to very different categories: taxes are so-called 'price instruments' and marketable permits are 'quantity instruments'. The distinction is not only theoretical. Many environmentalists are sceptical about economics and protest against treating nature as the subject of economic decisions. In contrast, marketable permits—especially cap-and-trade systems—put nature first: they set a limit to the scale of natural resource use, and then let market forces decide who takes advantage of using nature. This is an important (and unique) characteristic of marketable permits that needs to be emphasised.

The text refers to 'classic' implementations of marketable permits, including both early American experiments and the mature European carbon market, demonstrating that some systems are more successful than others. It also refers to less known initiatives—such as e.g. Polish attempts to introduce the instrument (Chap. 8)—to give students a more comprehensive view of environmental policy problems.

References

Baumol WJ, Oates WE (1988) The theory of environmental policy. Cambridge University Press. https://doi.org/10.1017/CBO9781139173513

Buchholz W, Reif C, Rübbelke D (2024) Foundations of environmental economics: an introduction to the economic analysis of national and international environmental challenges. Springer. ISBN 978-3-031-63480-2

Hanley N, Shogren J, White B (2007) Environmental economics in theory and practice. Palgrave, London

Lewis L, Tietenberg T (2019) Environmental economics and policy. Routledge

Phaneuf DJ, Requate T (2016) A course in environmental economics. theory, policy, and practice. Cambridge University Press. https://doi.org/10.1017/9780511843839.011

Chapter 2
Theoretical Foundations

2.1 Economic Advantages

In 1959–1972 economists laid down the theoretical foundations for applying marketable permits.

These are sometimes seen as corollaries of the Coase Theorem. The theorem states that when two agents that impose an external effect on each other can negotiate its allocation in a costless way, they can agree on its socially justified quantity. However, it seems that the idea of permit marketability emerged before Coase (who was honoured with the Nobel prize in 1991) formally stated his theorem.

In 1959, Ronald Coase prepared a report for the US federal administration which allocates frequencies to TV stations. In the report he recommended that federal officers do not issue any new permits if by doing so they would deprive some of the existing users of permits and hence expose themselves to criticism. Coase suggested that TV stations buy frequencies from those who have them but prefer to sell them rather than continue broadcasting their programmes. His conclusion was met with resistance, even though a similar logic is applied whenever any economic activities are started. In order to be registered, a firm needs to have an address—it needs to be located somewhere. In other words, it has to buy or rent real estate; nobody expects the government to give an address just because somebody else would have to be deprived of it. People tolerate the fact that the estate was perhaps purchased a long time ago and inherited several times since then.

The following year Ronald Coase (1960) published his famous paper outlining a theoretical solution of the allocation problem. Permits to use frequencies were supposed to be marketable. It is worth noting that the externality analysed by Coase had nothing to do with the fact that broadcasting may have an adverse impact on those who live near the antenna or on the recipients. The externalities analysed meant that using one frequency makes it more difficult to use neighbouring ones:

T. Żylicz, *Marketable Permits*, SpringerBriefs in Economics,
https://doi.org/10.1007/978-3-032-12133-2_2

frequencies allocated should not be too close to each other. Hence their number has to be limited. Any station using a frequency interferes with another station which uses a neighbouring one. Conflicts may be avoided by constraining the supply administratively (to make sure that frequencies used by various stations are not too close to each other) and introducing a market for frequencies. A generalisation of this idea constitutes the essence of the Coase Theorem.

Thanks to Coase, economists realised that a market rather than someone's administrative decision could determine what a firm should do if its actions had an impact on other firms. Although the allocation of TV frequencies is far from what environmental policies deal with, this is where marketable permits have been implemented successfully at a large scale. If a market is to determine something, the supply and demand sides need to be identified. It is easy to imagine demand for environmental protection. Yet is it possible to define 'environmental protection supply'?

Crocker (1966) gave a positive answer to this question in his path-breaking paper. He clarified that to this end one has to imagine the availability of projects that bring environmental improvements. In other words, if environmental protection is expected—e.g. in the form of emission reduction—it can be purchased (paid for). The term 'marketable permit' was not used, but Crocker's paper gave the first clear explanation of the idea.

The concept of marketable permits, called 'rights to pollute', was first detailed by John Dales (1968). Thus he is often identified as the inventor of the instrument.

The idea of marketable permits was outlined in the 1960s, but it was not quite clear if they could really deliver the expected results. In particular, it was not clear if they could indeed minimise environmental costs. A rigorous proof of this fact was provided by William Montgomery (1972). He proved the efficiency of permit trading even in the case of multiple pollutants as long as these did not interact with each other. The case of synergistic pollutants is explained in Sect. 2.5 below.

Montgomery referred to pollution control, but the model is general and applies to many other environmental problems, as explained in Chap. 10. Firm-level emissions can be substituted with individual harvest allowances (in fisheries), development rights (in landscape protection policies), water withdrawal allocations (in water protection policies), and so on. In every application there is an overall level of environmental use, established *a priori*, which is allocated among individual users.

The Montgomery model for a single market can be formalised as follows. There are n firms (numbered 1, 2, 3, ..., n) which emit the same pollutant (the multi-pollutant case requires a more complicated—vector—notation). The total emission is to be constrained by Z. An administrative entity gives the firm *i* a permit to emit β_i, while the sum of all permits has a cap (an upper limit) of Z (thus $\beta_1 + \ldots + \beta_n = Z$). Then the administrator allows permit trading so that each firm can minimise the cost of meeting the requirements (i.e. abatement cost plus the price of additional permits necessary to comply, or minus the price of unused permits). As a result of transactions, the sum of abatement costs will be minimised irrespectively of the allocation of the initial requirements $\beta_1, \ldots, \beta_n$.

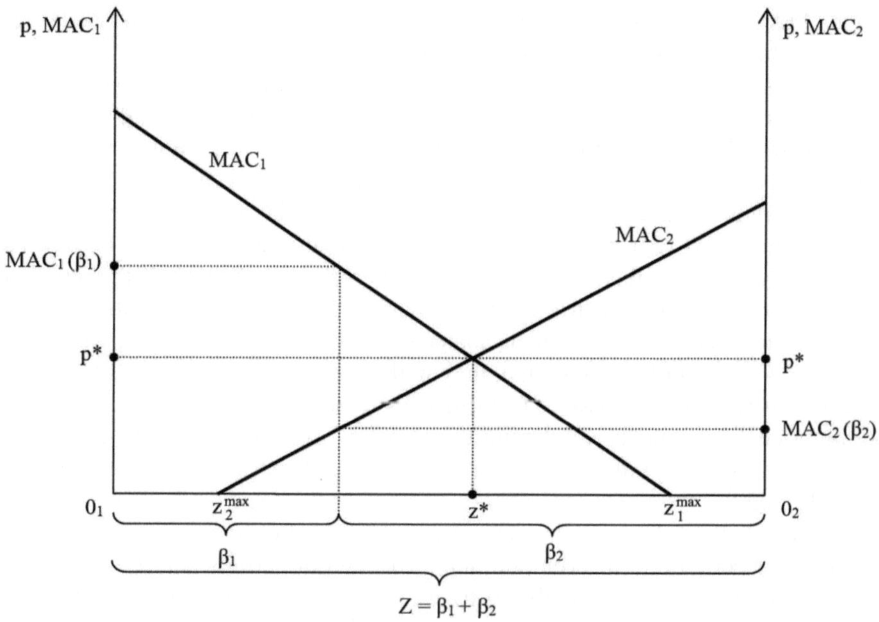

Fig. 2.1 Marginal Abatement Cost (MAC) curves for two plants

The proof of the theorem is fairly easy (it can be found in environmental economics textbooks, see e.g. (Żylicz 2004, pp. 62–63)). The graph in Fig. 2.1 illustrates its idea under the assumption that there are only two firms: 1 and 2 (its illustration in the general case would be cumbersome). The graph applies the convention used in such cases, namely all financial data (such as costs) of the first firm are measured along the left vertical axis, and for the second firm—along the right vertical axis. The horizontal axis is common for both firms but increases from left to right for the first firm, and from right to left for the second one. The distance between the two vertical axes (distance from 0_1 to 0_2) is equal to Z, i.e. to the total allowable emission from both firms combined.

In order to prove the theorem, let us assume (as is justified in many situations) that both firms are price-takers (they cannot manipulate prices). Let us also assume that their marginal abatement costs (i.e. bringing the emission to a given level)—MAC_1 and MAC_2, respectively—are decreasing: if the firms were to emit 0, this cost would be high, but if they were to emit more, the cost would be lower. Hence firm 1 would like to emit z_1^{max} and firm 2 would like to emit z_2^{max} (emission that requires no abatement effort). But then their joint emission would be $z_1^{max} + z_2^{max} > Z$, which is more than the administration allowed.

According to the permits that were issued originally, firm 1 is allowed to emit β_1 and firm 2 is allowed to emit β_2. The first one calculates that in order to abate up to β_1, its marginal cost would be $MAC(\beta_1)$, and the second firm calculates that in order to abate up to β_2, its marginal cost would be $MAC(\beta_2)$. As shown in the graph, $MAC(\beta_1) > MAC(\beta_2)$. Since these costs are different, perhaps it can be arranged that the first firm emits more (abates less), and the second one emits less (abates more)? Firm 1 is willing to buy a permit for an additional unit of emission as long as its price is lower than $MAC(\beta_1)$, because this would be cheaper than abating this unit. Firm 2, in turn, is willing to sell a permit for a unit of emission as long as its price is higher than $MAC(\beta_2)$, because the additional abatement required is cheaper (its cost is cheaper than in firm 1). Since $MAC(\beta_1)$ is higher than $MAC(\beta_2)$, a price can be agreed on that is acceptable for both firms.

Will they stop after this single transaction? Perhaps not. As long as the marginal abatement cost in the first firm is higher than in the second firm, both will have incentives to trade. Only when their abatement costs become equal, i.e. when they reach z^* (as a result of negotiations), they will no longer have incentives to change anything; it will not be possible to further decrease the total abatement cost. The permit price—economists call it equilibrium price—will be established at the level of p^*. This outcome will be achieved irrespective of the initial permits given to firms (β_1 and β_2).

In general, the following theorem can be proved. Let us assume that there is a market for permits for a given pollutant. The sum of permits is Z. Let us further assume that all firms (their number is n) are price-takers, their marginal abatement costs MAC_i are decreasing with respect to their emissions z_i, and the initially distributed permits are $\beta_1, \ldots, \beta_n$, with $\Sigma_i\beta_i = Z$. Finally, let us assume that in equilibrium the emissions from firms 1, …, n are $z_1^*, \ldots, z_n^*$, and the permit price is p^*. Then the total sum of abatement costs to reach the overall level of emission of Z has been minimised. This result does not depend on the initial distribution of permits $\beta_1, \ldots, \beta_n$.

Here is the proof of this theorem. If the distribution of $z_1^*, \ldots, z_n^*$ is an equilibrium one, then no firm has an incentive to sell a permit or buy an additional one. Thus for every firm *i* one of two alternatives must hold: either $z_i^* = 0$ and $MAC_i(0) \le p^*$; or $z_i^* > 0$ and $MAC_i(z_i^*) = p^*$. In the first case, the firm reduced the emission to zero and sold all the permits β_i, since the revenues from selling them were higher than the abatement cost. In the second case the firm has the number of permits necessary to emit z_i^*; the monotonicity of MAC_i implies that buying an additional permit (in order to emit more) would be more expensive than saving on the avoided abatement cost ($p^* \ge MAC(z_i)$ for $z_i \ge z_i^*$), and selling an additional permit (as a result of additional abatement) would result in lower revenues than the abatement cost incurred ($p^* \le MAC(z_i)$ for $z_i \le z_i^*$). It turns out that firms with positive emissions ($z_i > 0$) equated their marginal abatement cost. Given the adopted assumptions, this is a necessary and sufficient condition for minimising their joint abatement cost. The graph in Fig. 2.1 provided an illustration of the proof for the two firms ($n = 2$).

In the 1970s and 1980s, theoretical analyses were performed of the potential efficiency failures linked to the marketability of permits. The realism of both assumptions adopted in the Montgomery model—price-taking and rationality—was questioned. Numerous economic models assume competition leading to price-taking, i.e. the inability to manipulate prices. Yet one can imagine that an abating firm enjoys a privileged market position and dictates the price of its unused permits. Or it can be the other way around: a firm enjoying a privileged market position may dictate the price of permits bought. The price-taking assumption cannot be justified in these cases. Rationality, in turn, suggests that transactions will be carried out whenever permit prices are acceptable. But firms may behave strategically and ignore transactions that seem attractive, just to tease the competitor. Such problems could happen theoretically, but in practice they have not (Schwartz 2017, pp. 80–82).

There is abundant literature analysing complicated cases where firms are price-takers in some markets but enjoy a monopolistic or monopsonistic position elsewhere (e.g. (van Egteren and Weber 1996, Meunier 2011, Mansur 2013)). The energy sector has attracted much of the attention (Limpaitoon et al. 2014). Economists check whether 'emission trading' is likely to achieve an economic optimum (a socially justified outcome). Occasionally they detect that it is not, but the scale of this theoretical failure is much smaller than society's economic savings accomplished as a result of the marketability of permits.

A separate controversy is linked to the idea of property rights (permits have to be considered property rights of a certain kind). Some people would prefer stronger administrative control over private property instead of a market. Especially inheritance transactions are considered unfair in many circumstances.

Objections of another type are related to marketable harvest quota (see Sect. 10.1). Concerns are raised that efficiency improvements are achieved at the expense of indigenous people who do not consider harvest as a means of profit maximisation. In many regions, analyses of fisheries indicated that not only economic efficiency but also market concentration increased as a result of the transferability of permits. This led to displacing local fishermen by more efficient companies registered in distant locations (Davis and Jentoft 2001). Switching to more efficient (and aggressive) harvest policies resulted in the reduced resilience of ecosystems that used to be managed carefully and sustainably.

2.2 Environmental Advantages

Economists started to appreciate the benefits of marketable permits as early as in the 1960s. The advantages of such permits were soon recognised by environmentalists as well. Herman Daly (1992) pointed to an important argument for their uniqueness. He made a distinction between scale and allocation decisions. There are obvious objections to letting the market decide on a number of issues. Doctors would not appreciate it if ambient air quality was decided by pollution-emitting firms. Ecologists would not appreciate it if the country's forest cover was decided by lumberjacks. Spatial planners would not appreciate it if the density and height of buildings resulted from the commercial value of land only. Ambient air quality should take medical considerations into account. The country's forest cover should result from ecological requirements. The density and height of buildings should factor in landscape protection. In Herman Daly's language, these problems are examples of scale decisions. The scale should be determined by non-market factors. The market can decide (and in this role it exceeds alternative mechanisms) on allocation, that is what part of the scale can be used by which alternative users: which firms are to emit pollutants (as long as their joint emission does not exceed what can be tolerated by the environment); which trees are to be cut and which are to be saved (as long as the ecosystem survives); what compensations can be expected by those whom landscape protection does not allow to invest in dense construction or high buildings.

Daly (1992, pp. 191–192) refers to the following argument:

> *In loading a boat we also have the problems of allocation and scale – allocating or balancing the load is one problem (a microeconomic problem), and not overloading even a well-balanced boat is another problem (a macroeconomic problem). To avoid over-loading and sinking even a well-balanced boat we have a Plimsoll line defining an absolute scale limit. But the boat can be well or badly balanced even when the water line is far below the Plimsoll mark. And if the water line is above the Plimsoll mark, rearranging the load will be only a small help. Economists who are obsessed with allocation to the exclusion of scale really deserve the environmentalists' criticism that they are busy rearranging deck chairs on the Titanic.*

Marketable permits separate scale and allocation decisions in a perfect way. In the graph in Sect. 2.1, scale is represented by the total emission Z. Allocation, in turn, is how this total is distributed among the firms, i.e. z^* and $Z–z^*$ (in general: $z_1^*, \ldots, z_n^*$). Z is determined by the entity that issues permits. Yet z^* (or $z_1^*, \ldots, z_n^*$) is determined by the market. Thanks to this separation, the market enters where its role is unquestionable, and stays away from areas it is not supposed to decide on.

Daly (1992) emphasises that marketable permits indicate what part of environmental policy should be left to market forces and what should not be 'commercialised'. The scale (Z) is to be determined first in a non-commercial way. Once this has been done, the market determines how this scale can be used up by alternative beneficiaries ($z_1^*, \ldots, z_n^*$). The social cost of environmental policy is minimised as a result.

2.3 Marketable Permits Versus Pigouvian Taxes

From the theoretical point of view, marketable permits can be substituted with so-called Pigouvian charges with thresholds. The idea of a Pigouvian tax has been known to economists since 1920 (the publishing of the famous book by Pigou (1920)), but it took 72 years to realise that the tax could be implemented with thresholds (Pezzey 1992); if thresholds are applied, a Pigouvian tax is fully equivalent to 'emissions trading'. The tax rate should be set at p^*. Then the total emission will be Z, and firms will emit $z_1^*, \ldots, z_n^*$ (because their marginal abatement costs will not be higher than this tax rate). It seemed, however, that under the tax regime—in addition to paying for the abatement—firms would have to pay the tax. The total burden would therefore include p^*Z (i.e. more than in the 'emission trading' mechanism where only abatement costs were to be paid). The observation that a Pigouvian tax could be charged over certain non-zero thresholds implied that the equivalence of both systems was complete. In the case of marketable permits, the financial burden for firms depends on the initial allocation (as explained in Chap. 4); in particular, it depends on whether it is granted for free or whether firms have to pay for it. At the same time, in Pigouvian taxation any financial burden can be replicated by manipulating thresholds.

Even though the theory of marketable permits is much younger than the theory of Pigouvian taxes, it was implemented sooner. The theoretical relevance of Pigouvian taxes cannot be questioned—they are commonly used in economic analyses of environmental policies—but for various reasons they are rarely applied.

The need to separate scale and allocation decisions makes marketable permits a better environmental policy instrument than a Pigouvian tax. The theoretical scale Z of using the environment implied by the tax rate p^* is exactly the same as in the 'emissions trading' system (constrained by Z as the cap), but it is subject to uncertainty. If the administration makes a mistake in estimating abatement cost (a very likely case), the tax rate p^* will imply a scale that is different from the planned one. In contrast, in the 'emissions trading' system, the scale is *a priori* determined by the sum of permits, but there is uncertainty as to abatement cost. Which of the two types of uncertainty is more important depends on where priority is placed: the economy (allocation) or the environment (scale). Marketable permits suggest that scale is more important than allocation. Societies do not necessarily share this priority, and marketable permits are more widespread than Pigouvian taxes not because of preferring scale over allocation, but because of political reasons that are not analysed here thoroughly.

2.4 Psychological Concerns

Despite their advantages, marketable permits are sometimes criticised from the point of view of psychology. If the right to do something harmful can be purchased, users 'absolve' themselves of doing the thing they should be embarrassed with. Hence it is suggested that banning 'emissions trading' (and using non-marketable permits instead) would be more appropriate from the point of view of environmental protection since it would keep the pressure to reduce harm. Of course, there are psychological reasons for why the feeling of shame will not be weakened in such circumstances. On the other hand, polluters often use non-marketable permits so shamelessly that making these marketable would not really weaken anything. It seems that the advantages of marketable permits are so profound that removing the possible embarrassment is a matter of minor concern.

Besides, there are significant arguments indicating that marketable permits stimulate inventiveness and creativity better than other instruments (Milliman and Prince 1989). This is another reason why psychological concerns over marketable permits are not very convincing.

2.5 Theoretical Generalisations

The original ideas referred to single markets: a marketable permit was to regulate a single item (e.g. the emission of a given pollutant). The Montgomery model covered multiple pollutants but assumed that these did not interact with each other. All implementations worldwide dealt with single items. Yet in actual environmental processes, synergies are often observed wherein pollutants that happen to coexist either cancel out some of each other's effects or, on the contrary, reinforce their impact. For instance, tropospheric ozone (which causes smog and respiratory diseases) is formed—as a result of synergy—when nitrogen oxides and volatile organic compounds appear simultaneously. Both pollutants can be reduced separately, by applying marketable pollution permits. However, when they appear jointly, their combined effect is more harmful than if they are emitted separately. In contrast, alkaline and acidic substances discharged into aquifers may neutralise each other so that their combined effect is less toxic than for each of the pollutants alone.

The question arises whether environmental protection should be concerned only with single substances or with their synergic effects as well. Abatement of single substances can be effective even when they are tackled individually. Nevertheless, it is worthwhile to seek instruments that will achieve a combined effect at the least cost, such as marketable permits applied to single pollutants.

Endres (1985) raised this issue and observed that the answer depends on the shape of the function that describes the synergy. Żylicz (1994) generalised the Montgomery model. If pollutants regulated by marketable permits are not synergistic (they do not interact with each other), their joint abatement cost is minimised when the standard system is applied to them separately. However, if they are synergistic, then cost minimisation requires taking certain additional measures, and its results depend on additional mathematical assumptions.

Another complication stems from the fact that efficiency calls not so much for minimising abatement cost, but rather minimising the cost of reduced exposure. Some sources of emission can be characterised by a very low abatement cost (and hence offer unused permits at an attractive price), but—because of their location far from areas that are most sensitive to damages—their abatement does not have to be very strict from the point of view of environmental protection. Trading should involve not traditional emission permits, but 'exposure permits'. This conclusion was based on the experience with the US permits for sulphur dioxide (Muller and Mendelsohn 2009), as explained in Chap. 7. Other economists have also admitted that exposures rather than emissions should be traded.

Policies could therefore benefit from the excellent characteristics of marketable permits even in more complex circumstances. Nevertheless, there have been no attempts to apply them in such cases. It seems that applying marketable permits even with respect to simple pollution is difficult. Consequently, no government has tried to use them to solve more complicated tasks.

2.6 Coexistence with Other Instruments

Theoretically, marketable permits can coexist with other environmental policy instruments. Still, one should keep in mind their *raison d'être*. They are applied to save on environmental policy due to a cost-effective allocation of tasks. As a result of their application, a predetermined level of environmental protection (scale) is achieved at the least cost thanks to the market (allocation). The aim of marketable permits is not to improve the level of environmental protection. They are to limit pollution to a certain level (scale) and nothing more. By revealing that environmental protection is less expensive than expected, marketable permits may encourage setting more ambitious objectives (scales) in the long run (see Sect. 9.2), but one should not assume this in the short run.

Yet it is sometimes expected that marketable permits will reduce emissions below the agreed cap. People expressed their disappointment with the European system of trading carbon dioxide permits (see Chap. 7), especially after 2012. They complained that the emission was going down too slowly, even though in marketable permit systems emission is *a priori* determined by the sum of permits issued. The disappointment was associated with the fact that renewable energy (which does not lead to carbon dioxide emission) enjoyed subsidies. Despite the subsidies, carbon dioxide emission did not shrink faster.

The mechanism of this process is very simple. A power plant that wishes to increase electricity production invests in a windmill (or a photovoltaic farm), since its operation does not require buying an emission permit. But if the renewable energy is subsidised, the plant receives a grant to make the investment cheaper (even if the investment was to be carried out anyway). Hence the permits can be used to continue production that results in carbon dioxide emission. Therefore—despite subsidies—emission shrinks at the pace determined by the sum of permits, not faster.

Marketable permits can coexist with other instruments, but the outcome of these other instruments does not have to bring about the same results that could be expected in the absence of permits. Ignoring this fact may suggest that marketable permits are not functioning well, even though they are doing exactly what they were designed for.

References

Coase RH (1960) The problem of social cost. J Law Econ pp 1–44. https://www.jstor.org/stable/724810

Crocker TD (1966) Structuring of atmospheric pollution control systems. In: Wolozin H (ed) The economics of air pollution, W. W. Norton and Co., New York, pp 61–86. https://books.google.pl/books/about/The_Economics_of_Air_Pollution.html?id=hQ1EAAAAIAAJ&redir_esc=y

Dales JH (1968) Pollution, property and prices. University of Toronto Press, Toronto

Daly HE (1992) Allocation, distribution, and scale: towards an economics that is efficient, just and sustainable. Ecol Econ 6:185–193. https://ideas.repec.org/a/eee/ecolec/v6y1992i3p185-193.html

Davis A, Jentoft S (2001) The challenge and the promise of indigenous peoples' fishing rights—from dependency to agency. Mar Policy 25(3):223–237. https://www.sciencedirect.com/science/article/abs/pii/S0308597X01000148

Endres A (1985) Environmental policy with pollutant interactions. In: Pethig R (ed) Public goods and public allocation policy, Peter Lang, Frankfurt, pp 165–199. https://www.fernuni-hagen.de/umweltoekonomie/docs/endres_1985_environmental_policy_in_pethig.pdf

Limpaitoon, T, Chen Y, Oren SS (2014) The impact of imperfect competition in emission permits trading on oligopolistic electricity markets. Energy J 35(3):145–166. https://www.jstor.org/stable/24694922

Mansur ET (2013) Prices versus quantities: environmental regulation and imperfect competition. J Regul Econ 44(1):80–102. https://ideas.repec.org/a/kap/regeco/v44y2013i1p80-102.html

Meunier G (2011) Emission permit trading between imperfectly competitive product markets. Environ Resour Econ 50:347–364. https://link.springer.com/article/10.1007/s10640-011-9475-9

Milliman SR, Prince R (1989) Firm incentives to promote technological change in pollution control. J Environ Econ Manage 17(3):247–265. https://www.sciencedirect.com/science/article/abs/pii/0095069689900193

Montgomery WD (1972) Markets in licenses and efficient pollution control programs. J Econ Theory 5:395–418

Muller NZ, Mendelsohn R (2009) Efficient pollution regulation: getting the prices right. Am Econ Rev 99(5):1714–1739. https://www.aeaweb.org/articles?id=10.1257/aer.99.5.1714

Pezzey J (1992) The symmetry between controlling pollution by price and controlling it by quantity. Can J Econ 25(4):983–991

Pigou AC (1920) The economics of welfare. Macmillan, London

Schwartz JA (2017) Marketable permits: recommendations on applications and management. New York University, https://www.acus.gov/report/marketable-permits-final-report

van Egteren H, Weber M (1996) Marketable permits, market power, and cheating. J Environ Econ Manage 30(2):161–173. https://econpapers.repec.org/article/eeejeeman/v_3a30_3ay_3a1996_3ai_3a2_3ap_3a161-173.htm

Żylicz T (1994) Improving environment through permit trading: the limits to a market approach. In: van Ierland EC (ed) International environmental economics. Theories, models and applications to climate change, international trade and acidification. Elsevier, Amsterdam, pp 283–306

Żylicz T (2004) Ekonomia środowiska i zasobów naturalnych. PWE, Warszawa [Environmental and natural resource economics]

Chapter 3
Early US Implementations

The idea of marketable permits was conceived in the United States, and this is where they were first implemented. Textbooks (e.g. (Stavins 2003)) indicate three historic projects: (1) *offset policy*; (2) *bubble policy*; and (3) phasing out lead additives to gasoline. Combined, they allowed to save USD 5–12 billion on US environmental policy (Hahn and Hester 1989). The fourth early implementation, namely the Fox River cleanup in Wisconsin—perhaps because of its local scale—is not mentioned frequently. The following sections contain brief outlines of these implementations. The last section deals with intertemporal transactions called *banking*.

Some implementations can hardly be recognised as 'marketable permits'. Yet even though no commercial transactions took place before 1980, all of the policies referred to in this chapter relied on the following logic: polluters do not have to do what they are expected to do if they identify another polluter who undertakes the abatement on their behalf. After 1980 this approach acquired a legal framework which allowed polluters to sell abatement outcomes. There were several projects—e.g. 'Dillon Reservoir' (Carlin 1992)—where trading was permitted but did not occur. This chapter covers cases that are commonly recognised as early implementations.

3.1 Offset Policy

The US Clean Air Act of 1970 (EPA 2024c) introduced the concept of Prevention of Significant Deterioration. The concept implied that in areas where ambient air regulations were attained, all new and modernised emission sources should comply with strict and expensive technological requirements. In so-called nonattainment areas, no new emission sources were supposed to be located at all since air quality—which was already bad—would deteriorate

T. Żylicz, *Marketable Permits*, SpringerBriefs in Economics,
https://doi.org/10.1007/978-3-032-12133-2_3

even further. Administrators were not supposed to tolerate any new polluters. This, however, would preclude economic growth and doom such areas to economic stagnation. Neither politicians nor their constituencies would be willing to support policies that imply economic stagnation. Therefore it was contemplated how new firms could be introduced in nonattainment areas.

The idea of 'offsetting' emerged which meant reducing the emission from an existing plant in order to make room for a new plant. Thus, if an existing plant emitted e.g. X tonnes of some polluting substance, abating it by e.g. Y tonnes (so that the resulting emission was only X–Y) would create room for a new plant, as long as the new polluter was to emit less than Y. In the jargon used by economists, an 'offset' allowed to 'move' the pollution from an old plant to a new one. The administrator could then issue a permit for the new plant to emit less than Y. The plants would not trade the permits directly but would provide the appropriate documents to the administrator.

Of course no plant would make a spontaneous declaration to abate. If the emission was to be reduced somewhere, the promoter of the new plant should identify an existing one (where abatement costs are reasonably low), and finance an abatement project. The promoter of the new plant would have to carry out the project directly or pay the old plant to undertake it. The arrangement can be thus interpreted as 'the marketability of permits': the old plant does not use its permit fully, leaves the unused part for the new plant, and benefits financially.

Some analysts indicate 'netting' as an example of a separate environmental policy where permits are transferred from one place to another. 'Offsets' can be carried out within a single plant too. The Prevention of Significant Deterioration concept implies that a plant that is planning to modernise an old installation or invest in a new one should comply with very demanding technological requirements. This can be avoided if—by abating some emission in its old part—the plant demonstrates that in net terms the emission will not increase (hence the term 'netting'). Indeed this was a separate policy (involving a single plant), but its philosophy replicated the general idea of an 'offset' (involving two plants). The policy allowed extremely high cost savings, estimated at $525-12,000 million (in 1986 US dollars) (Harrison 1999).

3.2 Bubble Policy

The word 'bubble' has several meanings in English. In this context, the term refers to the space surrounding a polluting plant. A typical manufacturing plant has many installations that generate emissions. People who live in its vicinity do not care which particular installation releases which toxic substances; the only thing they are interested in is reducing their own exposure to the emissions. In other words, people see all of the emission sources as if these were in a bubble and would like to reduce their total outcome.

Inspired by this approach, American administrators who applied the 'bubble policy' (EPA 2024a) were expecting to have emissions reduced not necessarily from every single installation but rather from the entire plant. There was no formal emissions trading because all installations had the same owner (they formed parts of the same plant as was the case with 'netting'). Yet a rational calculation required that the owner of the plant determine where the abatement cost (per unit of emission) was the lowest. It made sense for investment efforts to be concentrated on these installations in order to save on the abatement cost where it was more expensive. By doing so, the owner was able to reduce the emission by what the administrator was expecting and pay for the abatement less than if reductions were to be made from all of the installations proportionally.

Even though nobody sold or bought anything formally, 'bubbles' worked like a marketable permit system because one installation shared part of its pollution limit with another installation. In some countries, environmental administrators apply this type of philosophy: instead of regulating emissions from every single installation, their integrated combined performance is analysed. European power plants benefited from this philosophy to comply with the demanding requirements of Directive 2001/80/EU which substituted Directive 88/609/EC (the so-called *Large Combustion Plant Directive*). Administrators did not look at the pollution emitted from individual installations but at the total impact of a plant (Klaassen 1996). This approach boils down to issuing strict permits where abatement is cheap, and issuing softer ones where abatement is expensive. In practice, however, information on abatement costs is hidden by those who run installations and only the market can reveal it. If administrators do not analyse the specific circumstances of each installation but determine the requirements for the entire plant, they *de facto* encourage 'emission trading' within a firm: various units of the plant negotiate with each other to allocate the abatement effort cost-effectively.

In some jurisdictions, administrators have always applied such an approach; they looked at the entire plant rather than individual installations. In 1979 the U.S. Environmental Protection Agency (EPA) decided to issue formal rules in order to allow firms to identify least-cost solutions to reduce emission (EPA 2024a). This new, flexible approach to regulation was expected to stimulate the development of new control techniques. The EPA referred to a study by DuPont which estimated that—without any increase in total emission—the new policy would allow the corporation to reduce its annual air pollution expenditures by 60% ($55 million instead of $136 million).However the actual cost savings resulting from implementing the 'bubble policy' are estimated at $435 million (in 1986 US dollars) for the entire country (Harrison 1999).

At the same time, safeguards were introduced to protect human health. Plants located under the bubble could not relax controls on hazardous substances in exchange for stricter abatement of less toxic pollutants. The policy allowed 'trading' emissions of the same pollutant (e.g. particulates for particulates, sulphur dioxide for sulphur dioxide, or hydrocarbons for hydrocarbons) only.

In principle, 'trading' was supposed to be confined to a single firm whose plants were located in the same area. 'Trading' between different firms located in the same area was allowed too, but required much more detailed documentation so that administrators could be certain that local air quality would not be adversely affected.

3.3 Phasing Out Lead Additives

Transition to lead-free (unleaded) gasoline—which was not universally available before—took place in many countries. Today, the crossed out ‘Pb’ symbol is a common sight at gas stations (the acronym ‘Pb’ stands for *Publium*, the Latin term for lead); fuels currently sold do not contain any lead at all. In earlier times gasoline contained tetraethyllead ($(C_2H_5)_4Pb$) which allowed engines to operate safely (the gas burned in carburettors did not damage the installation). As late as in the second half of the twentieth century a technology was developed that did not require such additives, although it called for some adaptation of engines.

By the year 2000 virtually all countries banned leaded gasoline. In the United States it was phased out between 1980 and 1986. Meanwhile, lead-free gasoline was already available there since 1974 to meet the demand from cars that were equipped with catalytic converters and did not tolerate lead additives. Still, other car engines required leaded gasoline.

It was estimated that the new technology was somewhat more expensive than the traditional one (a difference of USD 0.005–0.02 per litre of gasoline produced) (EPA 1999). However, this additional cost was lower than the savings of engine maintenance costs and much lower than the health-related benefits of reduced exposure to aerosols containing lead. Thus the phasing out of lead additives was not considered controversial in the USA.

Substances that contain lead are highly toxic. They damage the human nervous system, especially in children. Transition to lead-free gasoline was thus a necessity of environmental protection which required the oil processing industry to change the technology used. At that time there were around 300 refineries in the USA.

In 1980 the US government decided that leaded gasoline should disappear from the market within 6 years. In other words, it was announced that after 1986 refineries would not be allowed to add lead compounds to the gasoline that was produced. The 6-year transition period was established to allow refineries to adopt new technologies. In many countries around the world governments gave producers similar several-year transition periods to adjust to new environmental regulations, but this frequently led to failures. When checking compliance after the regulations were supposed to take effect (i.e. after several years), governments would find that nobody did anything. Yet it was impossible to shut down all the plants. Thus governments expressed their disappointment and announced new transition periods for the accomplishment of what should have been done earlier. Environmental protection suffered.

The US government had previously had such experience with other products and did not want to be cheated and unpleasantly surprised again. This time the government announced that it would be checking year by year if every refinery complied with 1/6 of its overall (six-year) requirement. Thus in 1982 refineries were allowed to add only 83.7% of the lead that was added earlier (100/6 ≈ 16.3); in 1983—only 66.4%; and from 1987 on—0. It is obvious, however, that applying a new technology with respect to 16.3% of the production does not make sense. Either the new technology is introduced (and one does not add lead at all), or it is not introduced (and one adds 100% of what was added before). In order to avoid 'intermediate' solutions (such as 16.3% of a new technology and 83.7% of an old one which does not make sense from the engineering point of view), the government announced that permits to add lead were marketable.

Some refineries were old and were planning to switch to new technology anyway, irrespective of the government programme. Some were new and therefore it made sense for them to wait a few years before undertaking a new investment. Refineries that switched to the new technology did not require permits to add lead and could sell all permits, since they did not use them. Those that were planning to apply the new technology in the future had to buy permits to be able to add lead as before, at least for the time being. There were 300 trading agents. The government expected the market to operate smoothly and there was no disappointment.

Leaded gasoline was eliminated in 6 years as planned. Effectiveness was achieved thanks to checking progress every year. Cost minimisation was achieved thanks to the marketability of permits. It was estimated (US EPA 1985) that annual savings with respect to the 'traditional' approach which precludes flexible investment schedules amounted to at least USD 200 million. Before 1985, lead addition allowances were calculated per litre of gasoline produced (so the total amount of lead depended on the production level), and after 1985 the government switched to absolute numbers. In environmental economic textbooks this programme serves as an example of the most successful early experiment with implementing marketable permits.

3.4 Fox River

Fox River is a small brook in Wisconsin that discharges into Lake Michigan. It is not noteworthy in terms of geography. Nevertheless it played an important role as the site of a successful experiment in marketable discharge permits (O'Neill et al. 1983).

There were as many as twelve paper mills located along its bank. There were also two municipal sewage treatment plans. Therefore there were 14 polluters whose joint pollution load was excessive for the local ecosystems. The director of the state environmental authority estimated the total pollution load (X) that the river was able to absorb without nature being destroyed. She then invited sewage abatement managers from the 14 organisations responsible for polluting the river. She announced that the total pollution load could not exceed X and that she did not care how this load was allocated. She left the invitees informing them that they could not leave or contact her until they agreed on an allocation. She promised to accept the allocation and to write permits for the implied quantity of sewage discharged by every polluter.

The 'conclave' lasted a few hours and resulted in the issuing of permits which were transferable (as long as their total amount did not exceed X). The river was cleaned up but experts are not sure if this was a successful implementation of marketable permits. From the formal point of view, the permits were not really marketable, since any change with regard to the user was subject to the approval of the administrator. Besides, there was just one transfer later on: a paper mill that was connected to a municipal sewage treatment plant did not need a permit anymore and gave it to the municipality. It is unknown whether polluters did not trade because there were some obstacles or whether the allocation was optimal from the very beginning and no improvements were needed. It is also unknown whether the initial allocation required some money transfers, or at least some promises. Nevertheless, the experiment was successful.

3.5 Intertemporal Transfers

Many systems have allowed the transfer within a firm of permits that are to be applied at different time moments. This is called *banking*. The term is sometimes used only with respect to depositing permits that are to be used in the future. An inverse transaction, i.e. using a permit now even though it was issued for future use, is called borrowing.

Both depositing and borrowing are especially justified when the permitted emissions accumulate in the environment and exert long-term effects, i.e. when people and nature react not so much to the momentary presence of a pollutant in the neighbourhood but when they are exposed to it permanently. Intertemporal transfers also enhance flexibility and can be beneficial for economic agents. Therefore, the possibility of banking is commonly expected, and indeed it often forms part of marketable permit systems. It was implemented for the first time in early American applications, and constitutes an indispensable element of many systems.

In principle, it was not included in the 'offset' and 'bubble' policies. Even in the initial stages of the lead phase-out programme, refineries were supposed to trade their surpluses and deficits within a quarter (they were not allowed to bank them). However, it soon became clear that sellers were expecting to be able to make transactions in a non-hectic way. Likewise, those who were anticipating the application of an abatement technology in the future wished to use beforehand the permits that they would not need later. Therefore, banking emerged spontaneously as a result of these early implementations.

There is no symmetry between depositing and borrowing. Depositing is not likely to threaten environmental protection. On the contrary, it implies that environmental protection starts earlier than planned, even though its future pace may be somewhat slower. Borrowing has different implications. Environmental protection is weaker at the beginning, since—as a result of using permits that are meant to be used in the future—firms can emit more than planned. Later on however, instead of undertaking the expected abatement, companies can announce bankruptcy, disappear from the market and fail to give back what they borrowed. Thanks to the permits 'borrowed' (which—*ex post*—turn out to be non-repayable grants), firms can increase emissions cheaply. When borrowing does not require costs in the form of a discount rate (and it is customary that discounting is not applied in such cases), the entire development turns out to be a simple cost-decreasing trick and competitors who did not apply it may regret not having done so.

Banking of permits is viewed unfavourably by some analysts who see it as reprehensible speculation. This is not an accurate accusation: permits should be treated by firms like any of their assets. The essence of management is to buy at a low price and sell at a high price. Hence it is not reprehensible to deposit permits when one expects their price to increase (so one will make money on selling), or borrow permits when one expects their price to decrease (so one will save on repayment). The fact is, however, that these expectations can be built on illegally acquired information, as has happened in the past (see Sect. 7.2). In such cases, it is reprehensible speculation.

In general, not using permits should not be assessed as reprehensible. Nevertheless, until now, the principle of *use it or lose it* is often practiced. It makes sense only seemingly. If a firm has a permit to use 400 m^3 of water but needs to use e.g. only 300 m^3, then it prefers to waste 100 m^3 rather than risk losing part of its permit in the future. This is not a pro-environmental solution. The marketability of permits (including their banking) helps not to waste natural resources.

References

Carlin A (1992) The United States experience with economic incentives to control environmental pollution. US EPA, Washington, DC. https://www.epa.gov/sites/default/files/2017-08/documents/ee-0216-1.pdf

Environmental Protection Agency (EPA) (1999) Implementer's guide to phasing out lead in gasoline. https://archive.epa.gov/international/air/web/pdf/epa_phase_out.pdf

Environmental Protection Agency (EPA) (2024a) Bubble policy. https://www.epa.gov/history/bubble-policy#:~:text=Under%20EPA's%20%22bubble%20policy%2C%22,or%20better%20than%20previous%20limits

Environmental Protection Agency (EPA) (2024c) Evolution of the Clean Air Act. https://www.epa.gov/clean-air-act-overview/evolution-clean-air-act#:~:text=The%20enactment%20of%20the%20Clean,industrial)%20sources%20and%20mobile%20sources

Hahn RW, Hester GL (1989) Where did all the markets go? An analysis of EPA's emissions trading program. Yale J Regul 6(1):109–153. https://core.ac.uk/download/pdf/72838173.pdf

Harrison D Jr (1999) Tradable permits for air pollution control: the US experience. In OECD Implementing domestic tradable permits for environmental protection, Paris, pp 23–51. https://www.oecd-ilibrary.org/docserver/9789264181182-en.pdf?expires=1734446783&id=id&accname=guest&checksum=3C2AE4D0C80E73FC826B637F0E1FC916

Klaassen G (1996) Emission Trading and the EU IPPC Directive. In: Marketable, pp 24–26

O'Neill W, David M, Moore C, Joeres E (1983) Transferable discharge permits and economic efficiency: the Fox River. J Environ Econ Manage 10(4):346–355. https://www.sciencedirect.com/science/article/abs/pii/0095069683900049?via%3Dihub

Stavins RN (2003) Experience with market-based environmental policy instruments. In Mäler K-G, Vincent JR (eds) Handbook of environmental economics, vol 1. Elsevier, pp 355–435

U.S. Environmental Protection Agency (US EPA) (1985) Costs and benefits of reducing lead in gasoline, final regulatory impact analysis. Washington, DC. https://nepis.epa.gov/Exe/ZyNET.exe/9100YK16.TXT?ZyActionD=ZyDocument&Client=EPA&Index=1981+Thru+1985&Docs=&Query=&Time=&EndTime=&SearchMethod=1&TocRestrict=n&Toc=&TocEntry=&QField=&QFieldYear=&QFieldMonth=&QFieldDay=&IntQFieldOp=0&ExtQFieldOp=0&XmlQuery=&File=D%3A%5Czyfiles%5CIndex%20Data%5C81thru85%5CTxt%5C00000021%5C9100YK16.txt&User=ANONYMOUS&Password=anonymous&SortMethod=h%7C-&MaximumDocuments=1&FuzzyDegree=0&ImageQuality=r75g8/r75g8/x150y150g16/i425&Display=hpfr&DefSeekPage=x&SearchBack=ZyActionL&Back=ZyActionS&BackDesc=Results%20page&MaximumPages=1&ZyEntry=1&SeekPage=x&ZyPURL

Chapter 4
Methods of Initial Allocation

Marketable permits can be bought and sold. Nevertheless, all transactions depend on what firms own, i.e. on the initial allocation of permits. There are two fundamental methods of this allocation: (1) grandfathering; and (2) auctioning. These will be analysed in what follows.

4.1 Grandfathering

As the term suggests, initial allocation refers to history. Firms receive permits for free (or almost for free), and their quantity depends on past emissions. It has been the most popular allocation method. Especially incumbents—polluting firms that used to receive permits for free—expect the same logic to be applied in the future. Newcomers who are planning to enter the market have a different point of view. According to the grandfather principle, they are to receive nothing. Since they need to buy permits from incumbents, their competitive position is weaker. Such firms would prefer to get some permits for free, but if they need to buy them in an auction, they believe that all competitors (both incumbents and newcomers) should be treated in the same way.

If the government tolerates the emission as it is, it gives permits corresponding to 100% of what firms emitted in the past. Typically, the government expects the emission to decrease. For instance, if the emission is expected to decrease by 10% annually, permits are given for 90% of the historical emission in the first year, less are given in the second year, and so on. In some systems, the government reduces the pool of grandfathered permits faster and saves some of them for newcomers or creates a reserve just in case.

Despite its popularity, the grandfather principle has a serious shortcoming. Namely, it is considered unfair in cases where some firms reduced their emission in the past while others did not ('historic emission bias'). Some firms postpone

T. Żylicz, *Marketable Permits*, SpringerBriefs in Economics,
https://doi.org/10.1007/978-3-032-12133-2_4

abatement in order to make their future tasks easier, because so-called baseline emission is high if nothing was done in the past and low if the emission was reduced just before the principle was announced. Pointing to this unfairness, firms that reduced their emission in the past demand to be allocated more than they emitted just recently.

4.2 Auctions

For many years, economists advocated for auctions as the fairest initial allocation method. Nobody gets permits for free. If a firm wants to have them, it has to bid for them. This system has three advantages. Firstly, unlike under the grandfather principle, it demonstrates to economic agents that the environment is not a free good; it has alternative uses, and therefore a price. Secondly, it provides budgetary revenues for the government. Thirdly, it does not grant anybody a privileged position.

Yet it has certain disadvantages as well. Most importantly, it introduces uncertainty related to prices. This is a general problem in a market economy though, since any prices can change rapidly and expose firms to unanticipated circumstances. This uncertainty can be alleviated by counteracting speculation, e.g. through emergency budget purchases or taxation. In many markets, transactions cover goods whose supply is determined physically and cannot be changed by means of an administrative decision. In contrast, the number of permits is considered arbitrary which leads to criticism of auctions.

However, if the separation of scale and allocation decisions is to be taken seriously, the number of auctioned permits should reflect what the environment can absorb rather than what is considered appropriate by some firms. The number of permits offered does not have to be arbitrary; it should result from environmental circumstances.

Revealing demand is another advantage of auctions. People learn the expected prices of permits on the secondary market: how much those who have unused permits (and want to sell them) are likely to charge for them, and how much those who have less permits than required (and want to buy them) are likely to pay. There are auctions where everybody can bid irrespective of the plans that they have regarding the permits being bought. The buyers include those who plan to profit from selling them but also those who plan to use them rather than to sell them. The buyers may include physical persons who buy a permit with the goal of not using but retiring it, and are proud that by doing so they contribute to the financing of environmental protection. In addition, buyers may include non-government environmental organisations that use membership fees to finance protection through the purchase of permits that are to be retired. The government may also participate in the auction. By buying permits (without planning to resell them on the secondary market), it can contribute to the financing of environmental protection to a larger extent than would be the case with the offered amount of permits. This amount may result from some earlier agreements but when the auction takes place the government may realise that it could have been lower.

The government has the right to decide on the total emission irrespective of whether the permits are marketable. Economic agents are always interested in the emission being as high as possible and may therefore claim that abatement is extremely expensive, demand high subsidies or threaten to go bankrupt. The prices determined in auctions reveal the actual reaction of firms and allow the government to assess the actual response of the economy to the amount of permits offered. If the price is not excessively high, the government can buy a certain amount of permits and reduce the emission to a larger extent than was previously planned.

4.3 Mixed Systems

Grandfathering has widely been seen as granting permits for free. Yet this does not have to be the case. Beneficiaries may pay something for the allocation. As long as the price paid is lower than that established by an auction, they are subsidised, at least partially. In the first departure from the traditional concept of grandfathering, firms pay for what they receive. In another departure, a part of the permits is grandfathered while another part is auctioned.

There are more complicated systems where the allocation is linked to some index. For instance, power plants are sometimes given permits proportionally to their electricity production. Let us assume that their production is accompanied by pollution, and the government would like to limit the emission to Y tonnes. If the total production is X MWh, then the allowable emission per unit of electricity is Y/X t/MWh. The more electricity is produced by the power plant, the more permits it receives. On the other hand, however, the higher the total electricity production in the economy, the lower the pollution permitted relative to 1 MWh. Therefore the outcome depends not only on what a given power plant does but also on what others do. Just as in an auction: the outcome depends not only on how a given participant bids but also on the bids made by others.

The initial stages of the US lead additives phase-out programme (Sect. 3.4) were based on a similar logic: lead additive allowances were determined per every litre of gasoline produced; in other words, the more gasoline a refinery produced, the more lead it could use.

Fuel suppliers in California are subject to another mixed system (Sect. 9.2). The totality of the fuels sold results in carbon dioxide emission. A maximum index of this emission per every litre of fuel is established so that cars can be considered more climate friendly. The index decreases every year; a schedule until the year 2030 has been announced. Each supplier has to achieve an appropriate index. Those who sell fuels resulting in excessive carbon dioxide emission (per litre) have to buy additional permits. The system does not establish any cap on emission because it is proportional to the volume of fuels used.

There are many ways to arrive at an initial allocation of permits. Grandfathering and auctioning can be considered as two extremes; some practical implementations rely on one of these. But there are also systems that combine the two. Economists are then expected to assess how much the economy has to pay for environmental protection and how this burden is allocated among the participating firms, some of whom may be benefiting from hidden (indirect) subsidies implied by partial grandfathering.

An initial allocation of permits can be performed in many ways. Irrespective of the mechanism applied, crucially it should not change at the time of trading. The transaction may not go through unless it is perfectly clear that the trading firm holds the property right to what it is selling. Likewise, if potential buyers are unsure of the assets owned by the seller, they may hesitate to make a decision. Economists who analyse marketable permits emphasise that allocation and trading phases cannot overlap.

Chapter 5
Main Types of Marketable Permit Systems

Textbooks distinguish two major types of marketable permit systems: (1) absolute limit; and (2) credit systems. The first one is often called *cap and trade*. Permit trading is common for both of them. Apart from this, they are very different. In what follows the two systems will be characterised.

5.1 Absolute Limit System (*Cap and Trade*)

It is closest to the original idea of marketable permits: the maximum scale of environmental disruption (e.g. the sum of allowable emission) is determined first, and the market determines allocation. Permits are used by firms that demand them more than others because their abatement cost turned out to be higher than elsewhere. Other firms prefer to sell their permits because their abatement cost turned out to be lower.

Of course, it is disputable whether the cap was determined appropriately. Perhaps it could have been lower (more ambitious) if abatement costs turned out to be lower than expected. Or, perhaps, it could have been higher (less ambitious) if the abatement cost—as revealed by the average permit price—turned out to be very high. Yet it was determined unambiguously.

The cap is seen as an absolute level of emission. Whether it is indeed strict depends on whether firms comply with what their permits allow. In actually implemented systems the penalty for non-compliance has always been so high that it would be inconceivable for a firm to emit more than it was permitted to. Besides, emission beyond what the permit allows results in the cancellation of an appropriate number of future allowances. Thus setting a cap is equivalent to keeping the emission within the limit.

The best known cap-and-trade system is the European carbon market (ETS) which has been operating since 2005 (see Chap. 7). The first US large-scale

T. Żylicz, *Marketable Permits*, SpringerBriefs in Economics,
https://doi.org/10.1007/978-3-032-12133-2_5

implementation occurred in the 1990s, as a result of amendments to the American Clean Air Act (see Sect. 6.1). The Fox River experiment (see Sect. 3.4) was based on the same principle, but its scale was very small.

5.2 Credit System

Here the word 'credit' has nothing to do with bank operations. It indicates that an emission reduction took place somewhere. The first doubts whether a reduction called for by environmental authorities actually happened appeared as the *offset policy* (Sect. 3.1) was implemented. These doubts referred to violating particulate matter concentration in ambient air, as the following (real) example demonstrates.

It is well known that a parking lot covered with gravel is a source of dust, and the resulting air pollution can be reduced if the area is asphalted. A US firm which covered its parking lot with a better surface applied to the environmental administration to have it acknowledge that the firm reduced particulate matter emission. The annual emission was in fact reduced by a certain amount but it was far from certain that this justified permitting a new plant to be located in the area. However, if the law was to be taken seriously, the owner of the parking lot could expect the newly sited plant to pay something for the right to be located in a non-attainment area.

The idea of the Clean Development Mechanism (CDM), a provision adopted in Article 12 of the Kyoto Protocol to the United Nations Framework Convention on Climate Change is even more controversial. CDM analyses whether projects undertaken by economic agents registered in so-called non-Annex I countries (i.e. 150+ countries that do not have carbon dioxide emission limits) result in emission reduction with respect to some baseline. If the emission reduction is acknowledged, a certificate, or emission reduction 'credit', is issued. The certificate can be used in an Annex I country (i.e. in one of the 40 countries that have binding commitments to reduce carbon dioxide emission) as a means of satisfying its commitment.

The trap implied by this idea may be explained using the hypothetical example of a refinery located somewhere outside of Annex I, e.g. in India. An investor announces a plan to build a refinery that will emit 0.5 million tonnes of carbon dioxide per year. This outrageous plan triggers indignation, but the investor explains that the emission cannot be reduced. Experts argue that there is a cleaner technology which implies the emission of 0.4 million tonnes only. The investor states that the new technology would increase investment costs by €1 million and would make the project inefficient. Experts indicate that this additional cost can be financed if an emission reduction credit of 0.1 million tonnes is obtained. Having obtained a certificate of emission reduction by 0.1 million tonnes, the investor can sell the certificate to a firm registered in an Annex I country. Having bought the certificate, the firm does not have to buy an emission permit (in 2022 the price of such a permit was around €100/t in the European

Union, so this certificate would have been worth roughly €10 million). The fact that emission in an Annex I country was not reduced by 0.1 million tonnes is of secondary importance. The more important outcome is that as a result of this unfortunate mechanism, global emission went up by 0.4 million tonnes.

Institutions that confirm 'credits' and issue certificates obviously try to reject projects that lack any prospects for emission reduction globally. The www site of the Clean Development Mechanism (CDM 2024) contains a list of approved projects. The hypothetical project from the previous paragraph is not on this list, but there are similar ones—involving for instance refrigerator production in India—where emission reduction seems equally controversial. Number 6916 on the list is a project of this sort which received an emission reduction 'credit' for 0.5 million tonnes. If a project comes from a non-Annex I country (where no emission limits are adopted), one can always claim that according to some scenario an emission reduction will take place. And if the emission from this country goes up, the project proponent should not be blamed.

5.3 Can Cap-and-Trade and Credit Systems Coexist?

They can, but the conditions for such coexistence are difficult. Procedures in cap-and-trade systems are clear: emission reduction credits (which can be sold) are created when a firm emitted less than it was permitted to. In contrast, in a credit system a certificate can be obtained if one convinces somebody that a reduction took place. Yet, if no emission limit is adopted, the reduction level is arbitrary. In the example from Sect. 5.2, the adopted level could have been e.g. 0.6 million tonnes—depending on the idea of a hypothetical refinery using old but cheap technology that proved to be convincing.

The refinery example is an absurd one, but there are less controversial ones. For instance, emission reduction 'credits' were granted to windmill investment projects in China within the framework of the CDM. Hundreds of windmills subsidised by revenues from selling certificates were constructed there. Windmills do not emit carbon dioxide, so it was impossible to use the threat of switching to more polluting variants. Yet it was possible to argue that electricity could be generated in a coal or gas fired plant and would result in emission. This argument allowed windmills to get certificates corresponding to the avoided emission of a traditional power plant. However, it is not possible to verify what happens with the money obtained from the certificates sold. If it is invested in fossil fuels or other activities that result in carbon dioxide emission, the reduction that was credited is doubtful. Part of the drastic emission increase in China (from 2661 million tonnes in 1992 to 12,667 million tonnes in 2022) can be explained by the fact that Annex I countries contributed to the financing of projects that were undertaken within the framework of the Clean Development Mechanism.

Despite their riskiness and doubtful effectiveness, credit systems have not disappeared. Taking into account the fact that cap-and-trade systems are difficult to establish, especially at the international level, many experts appreciate decentralised systems (including credit-based arrangements) which create networks that rely on the reciprocal honouring of certificates. Linking two cap-and-trade systems to each other is easy as long as increased emission in one can be compensated by decreased emission in the other. This is why there are good prospects for linking the European and Californian systems of limiting carbon dioxide emission. Conversely, linking an absolute level system to a credit-based one would be questionable. If the operator of a cap-and-trade system was to accept the fact that firms within the system can comply with the requirements by presenting certificates originating in systems where caps do not exist, the objective set would become meaningless. Firms reporting to the operator would demonstrate attestations that somebody achieved something, without making sure that this achievement did not lead to results that were contradictory to what the operator was expecting. Credit-based systems are reliable only when emission reduction is calculated with respect to a non-arbitrary reference level.

In 2015 the signatories to the United Nations Framework Convention on Climate Change negotiated a protocol—called the Paris Agreement—whose Article 6 aimed to identify the requirements that meaningful (not fraudulent) 'credits' should comply with. Certificates issued as part of the CDM are problematic. Still, at every conference of signatories some delegates demand that they be recognised universally, and since 2015 efforts have been made to render Article 6 meaningless. Limiting the role of CDM 'credits' turns out to be very difficult. Nevertheless the parties at the conference in 2021 decided that recognition of these certificates was time constrained (but still acceptable). In 2024 Article 6 was finally saved from future manipulations (but attempts to profit from fraudulent 'credits' are likely to continue).

Reference

CDM (2024) https://cdm.unfccc.int/Projects/projsearch.html

Chapter 6
The Grand Policy Experiment

In 1985 the American delegation to the conference of signatories of the Long Range Transboundary Air Pollution (LRTAP) convention refused to sign the so-called '30-Percent Protocol' which required countries to abate 30% of their sulphur dioxide emission. Environmentalists were upset but it soon became clear that the US government was planning an important programme to reduce emission anyway.

6.1 American 'Acid Rain'

'The Grand (Environmental) Policy Experiment' was a somewhat bombastic way of calling the country-wide sulphur dioxide emission trading allowed by the Clean Air Act amendments of 1990 in the USA (EPA 2024a). Earlier implementations of marketable permits were carried out at a smaller scale. Despite the modest name ('amendments'), the legislation was a real breakthrough as it provided an unambiguous framework for emission trading and started a true struggle against 'acid rain' (the contamination of air with acidifying substances such as sulphur dioxide). In the USA it is common for significant pieces of legislation to have misleading names; for instance, an important instrument to subsidise renewable energy sources was included in the 'Inflation Reduction Act' of 2022.

The new legislation allowed to address an ambitious task. During the subsequent two decades, the US emission of SO_2 was to be reduced by 12 million tonnes (from 23 million tonnes in 1990, i.e. by more than 50%). In the third decade of the twenty-first century, US power plants managed to emit even less than 2 million tonnes, i.e. much less than the total emission in Poland in the 1980s (Statista 2024).

It was clear that such a drastic reduction of emission would imply a significant cost—especially in the power sector. Experience from the 1970s and 1980s demonstrated savings that could be obtained through emission trading. But people feared that given the immense territory of the United States, from the Pacific coast

T. Żylicz, *Marketable Permits*, SpringerBriefs in Economics,
https://doi.org/10.1007/978-3-032-12133-2_6

to the Atlantic Ocean, there was a risk that if West coast polluters did not use their permits entirely, they would sell them to East coast polluters (or vice versa). As a result, so-called 'hot spots' (places with excessive emission) could appear. Consequently, in order not to allow transfers from one coast to the other, it was suggested that the USA area be split into two parts by the Continental Divide (i.e. by the Rocky Mountains range). The fears cited above were eliminated because polluters were supposed to hold two permits: one that was country-wide and marketable (aimed at protecting the entire continent), and a non-marketable local one (aimed at protecting the immediate neighbourhood). Consequently, polluters that accumulated many country-wide marketable permits were constrained by non-marketable local permits anyway, so the risk of creating a local hot spot did not exist. Ultimately the entire US territory was considered a single market.

The results proved to be outstanding. The emissions were reduced as planned. Economists estimate that the total abatement cost was decreased by tens of millions of dollars per year as a result of emission trading. The price dynamics looked disturbing though. Everything seemed to be stable initially, and permit prices never fell out of the $100/t—$200/t range (in 1995 US dollars). In 2004–2006 there was a rapid hike to $1,200/t, followed by a level of almost zero (Schmalensee and Stavins 2013). When analysed in correlation with political developments in the USA, this trajectory indicated that prices reacted not so much to ecological or technological changes but rather to what the administration did. Plants were guessing whether administrators would make abatement requirements more stringent or more relaxed. In particular, firms were expecting these requirements to become more stringent as a result of epidemiological research which indicated acute health consequences of particulate matter pollution accompanying emissions of sulphur dioxide. Yet, for political reasons, no legislative changes were made, even though epidemiological data would have justified a more ambitious scenario, that is a smaller pool of permits (to the extent possible, because purchased permits should not be confiscated).

Sulphur dioxide emission trading in the USA proved a great success. It also served as a model for Europe-wide trading in the emission of carbon dioxide. The European system will be analysed in the next chapter.

A closer analysis of US sulphur dioxide emission trading reveals that its success can be assessed somewhat less enthusiastically.

First, although the programme was successful, its original economic justification was problematic. The cost was estimated between 0.5 and 2 billion US dollars, and its purpose was to fight against 'acid rain' which was damaging American forests. The damages to ecosystems were estimated at USD 2–5 billion. Later on it became clear that the damages to human health were dozens of times higher than to the ecosystems. The health benefits of the programme were therefore much larger than its cost. However, at the time of its planning, the programme may have been considered controversial since the health aspect was not cited in its original justification.

Second, cost savings resulted not only from the marketability of permits, but also from an earlier deregulation of the economy. This caused rail transport to become cheaper, and improved the attractiveness of Colorado coal which was much less contaminated with sulphur than coal mined in the Appalachian region. If power plants (most of which are located in the East) had been forced to abate sulphur not in percentage terms but in absolute numbers, they would have switched to Colorado coal even without emission trading.

Third, the Clean Air Act amendments were signed by a Republican president. Later on, however, when Republicans lost the majority, they tried to disrepute the entire programme. Supported by some lobbyists from the Democratic Party, they tried to fight against desulphurisation achieved thanks to burning Colorado coal.

Fourth, in the twenty-first century, permit prices sky-rocketed when the government—inspired by epidemiological data indicating the health damages caused by exposure to sulphur dioxide—planned to lower the cap. Initially, permit prices remained low for many years. In 2005 they hit a sky-high level and later went down to almost zero. This dynamic was caused by legal controversies surrounding the cap in view of the medical research, and several court cases lost by the government.

Despite this, from the historic perspective, the US programme of marketable permits for sulphur dioxide has been considered a success. It resulted in a drastic decrease in emission, familiarised economic agents with the instrument, and—most importantly—brought the cost of environmental protection to such a low level that people are not frightened by the perspective of a financial catastrophe.

6.2 Inspiration for Other Endeavours

The success of 'The Grand Policy Experiment' had a number of consequences worldwide. Most importantly, it encouraged European leaders to apply marketable permits to comply with the Kyoto Protocol (see the next chapter). Trading carbon dioxide permits is even more justified than trading sulphur dioxide permits because in the case of the former the place of emission does not matter. No 'hot spots' are to be feared since carbon dioxide emission does not contribute to local air quality directly. Even the country of emission is irrelevant, so the European Commission designed a continent-wide market for emission permits.

As explained by economists (see Sect. 2.3), marketable permits are equivalent to Pigouvian taxes. In the context of carbon dioxide abatement, this means that emissions can be regulated either by marketable permits or Pigouvian taxes (called carbon taxes in this case). A review of policy instruments applied worldwide (Wood Mackenzie 2024) demonstrated that the former are more frequent than the latter. In many cases the encouragement came from the success of the 'Grand Policy Experiment'.

In 1994 the LRTAP Convention was amended by the Oslo Protocol (*Second Sulphur Protocol*). Even though the Protocol did not announce the marketability of permits, it introduced a number of provisions to achieve environmental objectives in a more flexible way. It abandoned the philosophy of uniform reductions (the same percent for each country), and called its signatories to apply instruments that were cost-effective. Perhaps the approach was inspired by what happened in the USA.

Apart from the global consequences, the marketability of permits has become a permanent element of American environmental policies. For instance, a policy to abate nitrogen oxide pollution that contributes to air contamination especially in the summer months (EPA 2024b) was adopted in North-Eastern states in 1999 (following earlier regional efforts to reduce air contamination). The area covered New England and several neighbouring regions. The problem was caused mainly by mobile sources, namely the emission of nitrogen oxides (NO_x) and other car exhaust gases that interact with each other forming ozone concentrations responsible for smog and acute health consequences. A non-government organisation called the Ozone Transport Commission (OTC) was established that is responsible for advising EPA on the development and implementation of regional solutions to the ground-level ozone problem. Historically the problem was addressed by abating so-called volatile organic compounds. Yet the OTC demonstrated that nitrogen emissions from power plants had to be reduced significantly in the five summer months of May through September.

It was clear that the cost-effectiveness of such an abatement programme required emission trading. The so-called *NO_x Budget Program* set a regional 'budget' (cap) on NO_x emissions from power plants and other large combustion sources—almost 1000 installations. The initial cap was 219,000 tonnes in 1999 and became 143,000 tonnes in 2003. Thanks to the emission trading programme, a reduction of over 60% (with respect to the 1990 baseline of 419,000 tonnes) proved to be feasible in just several years. The OTC identified the caps, while the EPA enforced compliance.

The programme was followed by the *Clean Air Interstate Rule* (CAIR). It covered 28 eastern states, and mandated reductions in sulphur dioxide and nitrogen oxide emissions that create damages in downwind locations. The targets were considered reasonable by the EPA. There were three separate marketable permit types: for sulphur dioxide, for nitrogen oxides, and for nitrogen oxides during 'ozone seasons' (i.e. May through September). Permits were largely grandfathered, but efforts were undertaken to avoid 'historic emission bias' (see Sect. 4.1), i.e. penalising coal-fired plants that had already installed pollution controls expected to be installed in the future.

The subsequent programme is the *Cross-State Air Pollution Rule* (CSAPR), launched after a court decision that identified some formal flaws in CAIR. Based on pollution migration maps, CSAPR requires certain states to reduce power plant emissions that cross state lines. It retains the overall idea of solving the problem in a cost-effective way. As before, there are three separate marketable permit types that have been proved to achieve cost-effectiveness of abatement. However, CSAPR gives the states the freedom to choose any method of allocating the cap to individual plants. Plants are not obliged to trade. Local governments are supposed to meet the overall cap by applying whatever methods. Due to the advantages of marketable permits, state governments have chosen the cap-and-trade solution.

On the other side of the continent, the *Regional Clean Air Incentives Market* (RECLAIM) was another programme aimed at improving air quality through marketable permits. Its focus was limited to Los Angeles and other parts of southern California. The *South Coast Air Quality Management District* (SCAQMD) was a local agency tasked with designing and operating this system that was meant to reduce sulphur dioxide and nitrogen oxide emissions from power plants. RECLAIM is considered a success, even though the prices observed on the market were very volatile. In 1994–1999 they stayed within the \$1000–\$2500 range; in 2000 they hit \$21,000, and in 2001 they sky-rocketed to \$41,000. This volatility was caused by flaws in California's deregulation of the electricity market rather than flaws in RECLAIM itself (Harrison 2004).

References

Environmental Protection Agency (EPA) (2024a) EPA history: Clean Air Act amendments of 1990. https://www.epa.gov/history/epa-history-clean-air-act-amendments-1990

Environmental Protection Agency (EPA) (2024b) Ozone Transport Commission NOx budget program. https://www.epa.gov/power-sector/ozone-transport-commission-nox-budget-program

Harrison D Jr (2004) Ex post evaluation of the reclaim emissions trading programmes for the Los Angeles air basin. OECD, pp 45–69. https://www.oecd-ilibrary.org/docserver/9789264015036-3-en.pdf?expires=1734458349&id=id&accname=guest&checksum=4451839E91B641AA794DAE5A9FFEA6F4

Schmalensee R, Stavins RN (2013) The SO_2 allowance trading system: the ironic history of a grand policy experiment. J Econ Perspect 27(1):103–122. https://www.aeaweb.org/articles?id=10.1257/jep.27.1.103

Statista (2024) Annual sulfur dioxide (SO_2) emissions in the United States from 1970 to 2023. https://www.statista.com/statistics/501303/volume-of-sulfur-dioxide-emissions-us

Wood Mackenzie (2024) Carbon markets: 5 things to look for in 2024. https://www.woodmac.com/news/opinion/carbon-markets-2024-outlook/

Chapter 7
The European Trading System

The acronym 'ETS' has two interpretations. The first two letters always denote 'Emission Trading'. The last one, however, stands for 'System' or 'Scheme'. The acronym is in frequent use. The ETS sector refers to plants covered by the system of carbon dioxide emission trading, and the non-ETS sector refers to all other emission sources. It is estimated that the ETS sector is responsible for 50% of European emission. Other sources—e.g. cars—do not have to acquire permits; they need to comply with other requirements. The ETS started to function in the twenty-first century, but its beginning can be traced to the twentieth century.

In the context of climate protection, so-called greenhouse gases (GHG) are often quantified in terms of 'carbon dioxide equivalent' (CO_2e). Apart from carbon dioxide, GHG include methane, nitrous oxide and other gases which—like freons—are called 'trace gases' since their concentration in the atmosphere is very small. They are more damaging for the climate than CO_2, but when their residence time in the atmosphere is taken into account, carbon dioxide dominates GHG. All of the other gases are recalculated in terms of CO_2e. The ETS covers GHG but carbon dioxide is its foremost target.

7.1 The Kyoto Protocol and the 2003/87/EU Directive

The third conference of parties (COP-3) to the Climate Convention took place in 1997. These are annual conferences which last two weeks and are summarised at press conferences. These press meetings allow the world to learn what was achieved when parties met. In 1997, the conference in Kyoto was supposed to culminate in the signing of a protocol which would commit Annex I countries (some 40 countries that were considered economically developed according to United Nations terminology from the 1970s; Bulgaria belongs to this group while South Korea does not) to limit their GHG emission. With just a few hours

T. Żylicz, *Marketable Permits*, SpringerBriefs in Economics,
https://doi.org/10.1007/978-3-032-12133-2_7

left to the press meeting, the signatories could not agree to anything meaningful. The US delegation stated that they would not sign any document unless there was a clause on emission trading, and the delegation of the European Union declared that they would not sign it if there was a clause on emission trading.

At the time, in Europe marketable permits were considered an 'untested American novelty', despite the fact that the international community had accepted them in another treaty ten years earlier. The Montreal Protocol of 1987, which limits the use of substances that deplete the ozone layer, provided that permits to emit these substances were marketable. In Europe, the reluctance to apply this instrument was so strong that perhaps the US delegation was expecting the protocol not to be signed at all and was planning to blame the European delegation for the failure of the meeting. The year before, the US Senate rejected any agreement of the Kyoto Protocol type by a unanimous vote. But the negative stance of the European delegation would have allowed to identify another culprit.

Things turned out differently though. Just before the press meeting—in order to avoid a complete disrepute of the Climate Convention—the European delegation gave up and agreed to emission trading. Consequently, it was included in three articles of the Kyoto Protocol. Article 6 stated that economic agents registered in Annex I countries could trade GHG permits. Article 17 stated that Annex I countries could trade GHG emission limits they agreed to comply with. Article 12 introduced the so-called Clean Development Mechanism (see Sect. 5.2), i.e. the possibility for non-Annex I countries to get a certificate of emission reduction that can be used in Annex I countries.

The US did not ratify the Kyoto Protocol (it was just signed—in bad faith—by the US delegation), which caused problems. The Protocol was supposed to come into force under two conditions. First, the number of ratifications was to be at least 55. Second, emission from Annex I countries that ratified it was to contribute at least 55% of the emission from all Annex I countries. Non-Annex I countries are not obliged to report their emission so it could not be referred to in a legal text.

The Protocol did not impose any binding commitments on non-Annex I countries so they did not hesitate to ratify it. Thus the first condition of its coming into force turned out to be easy. However—given the non-ratification by the US—the second one proved more difficult. It became clear that the Protocol would not come into force unless Russia (another large polluter from Annex I) ratified it. Without Russian emission the 55% threshold would not be reached.

Russia did not rush with the ratification. Knowing that the Protocol depended solely on its ratification, the country managed to utilise its unique negotiating position for a couple of years. The European Union pushed for saving the Protocol and accepted the conditions presented by Russia. Having achieved its political objectives, Russia ratified the Protocol as late as in 2004.

Anticipating the Russian ratification—and the Kyoto Protocol's coming into force—the European Commission established the ETS by drafting the 2003/87/EU Directive (European Commission 2024b) in 2003. It was to cover around 10,000 plants. In Poland—which acceded the European Union in 2004—there are some 1000 plants that meet the relevant criteria. They can trade with each other by selling or buying GHG permits. The permits were initially grandfathered for free. The pool of grandfathered emissions gradually shrank and auctions became more widespread.

The auction mechanism is considered controversial. On the one hand firms do not like it, since they would prefer to get permits for free, with historic emission taken into account. On the other hand, auction revenues flow to state budgets and—at least theoretically—justify lowering tax obligations. Ideas to centralise revenues by the European Commission triggered protests and have been abandoned. Hence permit auction revenues support national budgets.

It was not clear whether the Directive was to cover all European Union countries. Its preamble contains the following words:

> *(4) Once it enters into force, the Kyoto Protocol [. . .] to the United Nations Framework Convention on Climate Change and the joint fulfilment of commitments thereunder [. . .], will commit the Community and its Member States to reducing their aggregate anthropogenic emissions of greenhouse gases listed in Annex A to the Protocol by 8% compared to 1990 levels in the period 2008 to 2012.*
>
> *(5) The Community and its Member States have agreed to fulfil their commitments to reduce anthropogenic greenhouse gas emissions under the Kyoto Protocol jointly [. . .]. This Directive aims to contribute to fulfilling the commitments of the European Community and its Member States more effectively, through an efficient European market in greenhouse gas emission allowances, with the least possible diminution of economic development and employment.*

The European Tribunal explained that all countries—including those that planned to comply with the Protocol anyway—should participate since their participation would help other Member States comply.

7.2 Pilot Phase (2005–2007)

The Kyoto Protocol limited carbon dioxide emission (more precisely: GHG emission) in 2010. The Protocol accepted a certain level of flexibility, and defined the 2010 emission as the annual average from the five-year period of 2008–2012. In other words, it mandated the monitoring of this emission in 2008–2012. After 2012 it would become clear whether an Annex I country complied with its commitments or not. However, in order to see how emission trading under Directive 2003/87/EU was working, the European Commission decided to test its mechanisms as early as 2005–2007, calling this period the Pilot Phase.

Trading principles were not controversial. A more difficult element of the scheme was its initial allocation. This was to be proposed by Member State governments and confirmed by the European Commission. As will be explained in Sect. 8.3, the government of Poland tried to help Polish firms to participate in the ETS from the very beginning, but without much success. The first Polish permit sales were carried out when their price was low and declining.

The European Commission's very restrictive position with respect to Polish allocation plans was justified by the inflexibility of the Polish government which offered more generous allocations than were in fact needed. The Commission stated that the government of Poland—similarly to the governments of other countries that acceded the European Union in 2004—intended to give firms free permits that were excessive. The situation was more complicated though. So-called overallocation, which—according to the Commission—was 16.5% in the case of Poland, was even higher in the case of 'old' Member States (EU-15). For instance, it was 29.0% in Denmark, 25.9% in Finland and 19.4% in Luxembourg (Ellerman et al. 2007).

7.3 Phases II & III (2008–2012 and 2013–2020)

In Phase II, countries had to comply with the Kyoto Protocol. This turned out to be easy. The supply of permits was so high that their secondary market price was low and constantly decreasing. It was around €20/t initially but fell below €5/t (European Environment 2024). Financial analysts had no doubts that the low and decreasing price was caused by the excessive supply of permits offered in auctions.

In addition, in 2008–2012 the European Commission allowed the use of certificates issued through the Clean Development Mechanism since this was provided for by the Kyoto Protocol (Article 12). In sum, this was 1058 million tonnes of CO_2, i.e. roughly 10% of the five-year ETS market. The certificates issued in that period but not used were to be accepted in Phase III (2013–2020). After 2012 the European Commission announced that it would not accept any new certificates. Nevertheless, the market supply of permits was excessive even without these and resulted in their price falling close to zero. Ways were sought to increase the price by limiting the supply of permits. Banning CDM certificates was not sufficient. Authorities analysed ways to limit the supply of local (i.e. European) permits.

The confiscation of permits would be impractical and illegal. Its illegality would result from the principle accepted in civilised states that property should not be confiscated (apart from cases involving criminal offences), and owning more permits than required for ongoing operations is not a criminal offence. The impracticality of such confiscation would result from the fact that permits owned are registered on special lists where no distinction is made between what was grandfathered (perhaps for free) and what was purchased (perhaps for a high price). As long as confiscating something that was received as a gift has a different status, confiscating what was purchased would be subject to a cumbersome compensation procedure. Hence confiscating permits owned by firms was not an option.

At the same time, confiscating something not owned by private economic agents was a feasible option. It was possible to confiscate a part of the permits that were to be offered by governments in auctions. This was consistent with property rights because it affected something that was to be sold by governments, not by private entities. European treaties do not preclude such a procedure. If any member states had insisted against such a solution strongly, it would not have been implemented.

Since there was no opposition, the European Commission decided to authorise only part of what had originally been planned. The operation was called *back-loading*. This meant withdrawing a certain pool of permits from auctions. It was decided that less permits would be offered in auctions according to the following schedule:

- 400 million tonnes less in 2014
- 300 million tonnes less in 2015
- 200 million tonnes less in 2016

Overall, permits corresponding to 900 million tonnes of carbon dioxide were removed from the market. The operation worked. Permit prices started to rise and in 2022 surpassed the level of €100/t. Prices decreased slightly later on but remain close to €100/t (Sect. 7.5).

The fate of backloaded permits was to be settled afterwards. They were not confiscated officially but deposited as the so-called *Market Stability Reserve*. When the market price of a permit turns out to be excessively high, backloaded permits can be used to increase the supply. It is not clear, however, what price is 'excessively high'. For some agents the price of €100/t is already excessively high. For others it is not, and therefore does not justify using the *Market Stability Reserve*. According to calculations as presented by Nordhaus (2007), an economically justified price (in 2005 US dollars) was between \$30/tC and \$40/tC in 2015; it gradually went up afterwards to reach \$200/tC by the end of the twenty-first century. Recalculated with respect to CO_2, this corresponded to \$8-11/tCO_2 in 2015 and \$55/tCO_2 by the end of the twenty-first century. In contrast, according to Stern (2006), in the same period, justified prices changed from \$260/tC to \$980/tC, i.e. from \$98/tCO_2 to \$267/tCO_2. The difference between Nordhaus' and Stern's estimations is dramatic. According to Stern, permit prices in the ETS were justified, and according to Nordhaus they were excessive and thus called for using the reserve.

Later on a principle was adopted that the reserve was to be used (up to 75 million tonnes) if the average price for the six preceding calendar months was more than 2.4 times the average recorded for the preceding two-year reference period. Yet after 2020 the price was high but stable.

7.4 Phase IV (2021–2030) and ETS2

Since 2020, ETS has become an obvious and important instrument of European environmental policy. The gradual disappearance of grandfathering which was substituted by auctions is considered controversial but acceptable. European governments rely on professional financial organisations (like the European Energy

Exchange, EEX, in Frankfurt) to run auctions. The high revenues that flow to national budgets have perhaps provided a new powerful argument to accept this instrument which is not considered an 'American novelty' anymore.

The European Commission set a target of reducing GHG emission by at least 55% by 2030, compared to 1990 levels. This will enable the EU to become the first 'climate-neutral' continent by 2050. Even though the 55% figure does not confine to abatement—it includes so-called removals, i.e. emission reduction credits obtained by capturing some carbon dioxide from the atmosphere—it turned out to be very ambitious. Backloading proved to be insufficient to meet this goal. In addition to tightening the cap of the ETS, efforts were made to include more industries in the trading sector, and to control revenues from auctions. Several Directives (e.g. 2018/410) and Regulations (e.g. 2023/955) were adopted in order to abate carbon dioxide more than was initially planned.

At the same time a union solidarity mechanism was created, perhaps serving as an admission that a lower cap would imply very different relative economic burdens in various European countries. ETS auction revenues collected by wealthier governments were to contribute to the newly established Modernisation Fund. The Fund is to support activities linked to a so-called 'Just Transition', i.e. transition to a low-carbon economy in a way that addresses a number of its social implications. Central and Eastern European countries are the beneficiaries of the Fund. Poland's share was determined to be 43.41% of its disbursements. Other countries enjoy much lower shares (ranging from 1.44% for Latvia to 15.59% for the Czech Republic). From 2026 onwards, an additional fund—called the Social Climate Fund—will operate to support the Just Transition.

With aviation and maritime emitters included (since 2012 and 2024, respectively), ETS started to be even more comprehensive. A new name—ETS2—was adopted to emphasise that completely new entities would be required to participate in trading. This new system covers CO_2 emissions from fuel combustion in buildings, road transport and additional sectors (mainly small industry not covered by the ETS). Unlike the original ETS, the ETS2 affects upstream suppliers. It is fuel suppliers (producers or sellers), rather than end consumers such as households or car users, who are required to take into account their hypothetical emissions at a later stage. Regulated under the ETS2, these entities are required to submit sufficient allowances (purchased at auctions) to cover their implied emissions. The ETS2 2030 cap will bring emissions down by 42% compared to 2005 levels.

The European Commission also had to acknowledge that ambitious European targets implied a risk of massive 'carbon leakage', i.e. the promotion of foreign economic activities that result in moving the emission elsewhere and in unfair competition from international firms that operate in economies free from such targets. In order to deal with 'carbon leakage', the Commission is working on the Carbon Border Adjustment Mechanism (CBAM) (European Commission 2024a) and has introduced measures aimed at supporting European firms that have to buy ETS permits.

All importers of goods covered by CBAM will have to buy special certificates. The price of the certificates will depend on the auction price of EU ETS allowances. Importers will declare the emissions embodied in their imports and submit the corresponding number of certificates. If importers prove that a certain carbon price has already been paid during the production of the imported goods, the corresponding amount can be deducted. This provision will encourage moving away from imports originating in countries that do not have carbon markets similar to the European Union. It will become obligatory for all member states.

While theoretically justified, the new legislation is likely to trigger massive controversies caused by difficulties in calculating the carbon price paid in the exporting country. Non-Annex I countries have neither binding commitments to abate nor instruments to charge carbon prices similar to what is observed in Europe. Therefore—at least at the beginning—only raw materials (such as fuels or ores) will be subject to the mechanism. More specifically, the European Commission plans to cover cement, iron, steel, aluminium, fertilisers, electricity and hydrogen. More sophisticated products—like computers and cars—are much more difficult to analyse since their production is likely to originate in dozens of countries. The European Commission is aware of the problem, and allows using estimated numbers for complex goods (provided that the hypothetical number accounts for less than 20% of the total embodied emission).

In order to respond to exporters' concerns, the Commission plans to operate a special CBAM Registry where exporting firms can upload their emission figures ensuring the confidentiality of business-sensitive data and streamlining the calculations.

In the meantime—i.e. before CBAM becomes fully operational—ETS industries identified as 'Energy Intensive Trade Exposed' (EITE) will benefit from some forms of grandfathering and subsidies aimed at lowering the burden of permit purchases.

7.5 Firm-Level Responses to ETS

Firm-level responses to ETS are interesting. Entrepreneurs would prefer to operate without any permits. But European firms are aware that climate protection policies imply constraints on carbon dioxide emission. Therefore, if firms are to be regulated, the marketability of permits provides a general opportunity to improve efficiency. Yet companies take advantage of this in a number of different ways. At the same time, grandfathering creates additional benefits.

Abrell et al. (2022) summarised the first decade of European trading to find that firms' behaviour was related to some of their characteristics. In addition, the occurrence of transaction costs was demonstrated.

A more detailed study of German manufacturers by Hintermann et al. (2024) shows that a lot depends on whether firms can 'pass through' their increased costs to buyers. As a rule, electricity producers are less exposed to international competitors than other agents (Fell et al. 2015), so they can. Consequently, they did not need to be subsidised through grandfathering for free, but they were (at least in the first two ETS phases). The number of grandfathered permits depends on the assessment whether a firm can or cannot accommodate the increased production cost. The German study demonstrated that permit allocations did not result in adverse economic consequences for firms. On the contrary, some of them even benefited from ETS.

An interesting phenomenon was observed in the Pilot Phase. Firms preferred to 'trade' with themselves. They were eager to borrow from their future allowances, but analysts considered this to be a predictable way of reducing asymmetric information and transaction costs—something typical for markets in their early stages. Later on it turned out that there was a sort of 'home-bias', i.e. a reluctance to trade with foreign firms even when it seemed profitable (Jaraitė-Kažukauskė and Kažukauskas 2015). Hintermann and Ludwig (2023)—who also demonstrated 'home-bias'—explained that this could be an effect of transaction costs that are difficult to document.

7.6 ETS and the Rest of the World

The ETS is confined to the countries of the European Union. Some Annex I countries which are not member states of the EU but accept its policy (e.g. Norway) participate in the ETS on a voluntary basis. Since 2020, the Swiss ETS has been linked to the EU scheme. Following Brexit, UK firms do not have to participate in the ETS. Nevertheless, power plants located in Northern Ireland continue to do so.

Non-Annex I countries cannot join the scheme, since they do not have emission limits (caps). They can only apply for Clean Development Mechanism certificates (see Sects. 5.2 and 5.3) which—because of obvious conditions required by the ETS—have always had lower prices than permits originating in Europe. New certificates have been prohibited entirely in the ETS since 2013. In practice, the certificates are purchased rarely and on a voluntary basis (usually by private persons) to demonstrate one's contribution to climate protection in less developed countries.

The potential attractiveness of the ETS seems to be significant. If a non-Annex I firm reduces its carbon dioxide (or GHG) emission, it would be interested in selling the outcome at an attractive price. For the moment, it can only apply for a certificate whose market price is low. Its ETS price would be much higher, but the ETS operates in countries with emission limits. As long as the European Union is serious about its carbon dioxide cap, high ETS prices allow to hope that firms registered in non-Annex I countries will press their governments to adopt emission limits.

References

Abrell J, Cludius J, Lehmann S, Schleich J, Betz R (2022) Corporate emissions-trading behaviour during the first decade of the EU ETS. Environ Resour Econ 83(1):47–83. https://doi.org/10.1007/s10640-021-00593-7

Ellerman AD, Büchner BK, Carraro C (eds) (2007) Allocation in the European emissions trading scheme. Rights, rents and fairness, Cambridge University Press. https://cadmus.eui.eu/handle/1814/15699

European Commission (2024a) Carbon border adjustment mechanism. https://taxation-customs.ec.europa.eu/carbon-border-adjustment-mechanism_en

European Commission (2024b) Directive 2003/87/EC. https://eur-lex.europa.eu/legal-content/EN/TXT/PDF/?uri=CELEX:32003L0087

European Environment Agency (2024) Emissions, allowances, surplus and prices in the EU ETS, 2005–2020. https://www.eea.europa.eu/data-and-maps/figures/emissions-allowances-surplus-and-prices

Fell H, Hintermann B, Vollebergh H (2015) Carbon content of electricity futures in Phase II of the EU ETS. Energy J 36(4):61–83. https://doi.org/10.5547/01956574.36.4.hfel

Hintermann B, Ludwig M (2023) Home country bias in international emissions trading: evidence from the EU ETS. Resour Energy Econ 71:101336. https://doi.org/10.1016/j.reseneeco.2022.101336

Hintermann B, Žarković M, Picard L, Di Maria C, Wagner U (2024) The effect of climate policy on productivity and cost pass-through in the German manufacturing sector. Working papers from Faculty of Business and Economics–University of Basel. https://www.dropbox.com/scl/fo/zcrmdxqwssektp6b4wt2n/AGE_nqk8h-4wtAQZgk2F3VQ?dl=0&e=1&preview=Hintermann_et_al_2024.pdf&rlkey=gcnykal2dlg8rw1162nbowrmt

Jaraitė-Kažukauskė J, Kažukauskas A (2015) Do transaction costs influence firm trading behaviour in the European emissions trading system? Environ Resour Econ 62(3):583–613. https://link.springer.com/article/10.1007/s10640-014-9831-7

Nordhaus WD (2007) A review of the Stern Review on the economics of climate change. J Econ Lit 45(3):686–702. https://www.aeaweb.org/articles?id=10.1257/jel.45.3.686

Stern N (2006) The economics of climate change: the Stern Review. Cambridge University Press. https://webarchive.nationalarchives.gov.uk/ukgwa/20100407172811/https:/www.hm-treasury.gov.uk/stern_review_report.htm

Chapter 8
Polish Attempts to Introduce Marketable Permits

The collapse of the central planning system in 1989 allowed a new approach to environmental protection and led to the elaboration of a new environmental policy. The relevant government document (MOSZNiL 1990a) included the following paragraph:

> *Economic instruments will serve to minimise the social costs of environmental protection thanks to an efficient differentiation of abatement tasks. Agents whose abatement costs are lower should be given more stringent requirements. In practice, this principle will be implemented by marketable permits. Emission (or discharge) rights allocated to one agent can be sold to another, subject to the approval of the entity that determined the rights.* [p. 13]

In a document (MOSZNiL 1990b) devoted to economic instruments, this principle was outlined in greater detail.

> *Subject to specific legal constraints, administrators authorised to issue emission or discharge permits may choose from several methods to plan and implement environmental protection. In particular – depending on their knowledge and staff experience – they can choose any of the following four methods, or apply their combination. First, they may find it sufficient to enforce national emission standards (including technological requirements). Second, they may issue administrative decisions to require stricter standards for particular environment users to comply with, without the possibility of violating these in exchange for financial compensation. Third, they may regulate access to the environment through a system of fees and fines that currently apply. Fourth, they may establish 'permit markets' so that an environmental user can transfer some or all of their rights to emit or discharge to another user of the same airshed or watershed; the administrators confirm the acceptability of every transaction of this type.* [p. 8]

Many Polish decision-makers became convinced about the merits of this instrument which at the time had not been applied in Europe. Still, doubts emerged whenever they contacted officials from other European countries who recommended not accepting 'unverified American novelties'. These were not 'unverified novelties', because successful American implementations were numerous. In addition, reservations against marketable permits (just as against any reforms) could

T. Życzicz, *Marketable Permits*, SpringerBriefs in Economics,
https://doi.org/10.1007/978-3-032-12133-2_8

largely be summarised as: 'perhaps it worked somewhere, but it will never work in Poland'. Hence there was a need to arrange an experiment to demonstrate that this could work in Poland as well.

8.1 The Chorzów Project

Experts sought a place in Poland where transferring emission from one source to another would allow a quick and cheap improvement. The place was to comply with several conditions. First, environmental quality was to be bad—an easy requirement in Poland in 1990. Second, the area was to be administered by a competent and dedicated local government—a requirement that could be met in a number of locations. An additional condition was that local polluters were to be characterised by visibly different abatement costs. Even slight cost differences would justify the transferability of permits, but the idea was to demonstrate significant cost savings.

Chorzów was selected. Ambient air in the town was considered as one of the most contaminated in the country. There were two stacks in its very centre. One belonged to the Kosciuszko steel mill and the other to the Chorzów power plant. Their emissions exposed people to unprecedented pollution. Both plants had abatement programmes likely to bring environmental improvements over the following few years. The programmes offered little relief to the parents of small children. They were not satisfied with improvements expected to take place sometime in the future; they expected to see improvements immediately.

As seen in Table 8.1, the pollution loads emerging from both plants were similar. The people in Chorzów did not care which plant did what as long as the total emission was cut at least by half. Emission reduction opportunities in the steel mill were relatively cheap while those in the power plant were more expensive. Hence the abatement cost difference condition was satisfied. Economic efficiency required the steel mill to abate more but regulations did not allow this; if the pollution was to be cut by half, then both plants were to be given permits for 50% of their prior emission since the so-called background concentration of air pollutants was the same for both. The regional administrator in Katowice worked on

Table 8.1 Emission of selected pollutants in Chorzów in 1990 (tonnes)

	Steel mill	Power plant
Particulate matter	4.28	5.067
Carbon monoxide	16.951	200
Sulphur dioxide	3.02	3.071
Nitrogen dioxide	1.716	561
Aliphatic hydrocarbons	492	71
Aromatic hydrocarbons	282	8

Source Records of the regional environmental office in Katowice

preparing the appropriate permits. The expectation was that his decision would lead to appeals filed by both plants, and that the bureaucratic procedure would continue over the following few years.

Yet the administrator was encouraged by the Minister of Environment to make an 'experiment' and to write two different permits for the neighbouring plants: a more stringent one for the steel mill, and a softer one for the power plant. In order to comply with the relevant regulations, it had to be argued that background concentrations were different for both plants. If these decisions were legally challenged, they could have been lifted as something on the verge of legality. They were not. The decisions were not sued by environmental non-government organisations, perhaps thanks to intense cooperation between the Ministry and the club of environmental journalists ('Ekos'). The steel mill, which could have considered its stringent permit as unfair, did not sue either. The steel mill received a subsidy from the regional environmental fund.

From the formal point of view the permits were not marketable; regulations did not allow this. Therefore, two non-marketable permits were issued for the plants. They were not symmetric though. The plant that got the more lenient permit had to pay higher emission fees to the regional environmental fund, and money flowed to the one that got the more stringent permit. In a sense, the former paid the latter—not directly but through the fund. The one that emitted more (i.e. abated less) paid the one that emitted less (i.e. abated more). The flow of money resembled what would have happened in a system of emission trading. Hence it can be concluded that—metaphorically—the permits were marketable.

The experiment resulted in a spectacular outcome. The emission was cut by more than half almost immediately. Table 8.2 summarises this result.

Thanks to the project, town inhabitants benefitted from rapidly improved ambient air quality. Neighbouring municipalities requested the regional administrator to issue similar non-symmetrical permits. The administrator replied that he was not going to replicate the Chorzów decisions because that was just an experiment. If the procedure was to be repeated routinely, someone almost certainly would have challenged his decisions legally and the outcome of court proceedings would have been uncertain, since issuing non-symmetric permits did

Table 8.2 Emission of selected pollutants in Chorzów in 1992

	Steel mill		Power plant	
	tonnes	1992/1990(%)	tonnes	1992/1990(%)
Particulate matter	517	12	4.028	80
Carbon monoxide	47	0.3	1.141	570
Sulphur dioxide	972	32	3.226	105
Nitrogen dioxide	769	45	1.782	318
Aliphatic hydrocarbons	0	0	71	100
Aromatic hydrocarbons	0	0	9	112

Source Records of the regional environmental office in Katowice

not have a clear regulatory status. It seemed that an unquestionable legal foundation would be established soon. It was not, but firms—especially in the energy sector—became strongly convinced that marketable permits could lower the cost of environmental protection.

8.2 Legislative Attempts in the 1990s

Due to political instability, it was difficult to expect the government to prepare legislative amendments quickly. Such amendments were initially prepared at the Ministry of Environment within the framework of a PHARE project (Atmoterm 1996). Polish experts were supported by American colleagues (Stavins and Żylicz 1995). European experts explained how marketable permits could be made consistent with the European Union *acquis* (Marketable 1996). However, there was no political will to use the momentum, and the plans were abandoned (Żylicz 1999).

A few years later, power plants decided to take the initiative and prepare legislative amendments independently. To this end, the Polish Power Plants Economic Society (a private entity) commissioned the preparation of all necessary documents (EnergSys 2003). Academics collaborated with practitioners. As a result, the legislative amendments prepared were both theoretically sound and politically feasible, and addressed all practical issues. The power plants were right to expect that sulphur dioxide would inevitably have to be abated. At the same time they knew that marketable permits could lower the overall abatement cost. Therefore they collected money to finance the preparation of the amendments.

Yet the amendments were never implemented. The legislative proposals were not taken up by political parties. They had different priorities at that time.

8.3 Participation in European Emission Trading

Attempts to use marketable pollution permits to cost effectively abate sulphur dioxide and other local pollutants did not succeed. In the twenty-first century European countries started to apply marketable pollution permits in carbon dioxide abatement. The establishment of this market in Europe is so remarkable that a separate chapter was devoted to it. Here the focus is on Polish developments only. They are rooted in events that took place earlier, i.e. in the 1990s.

The European Commission drafted a breakthrough directive to comply with the Kyoto Protocol (Directive 2003/87/EU; see Sect. 7.2). It was not clear, however, which countries were covered by its provisions. The wording of the Directive caused the government of Poland to ask for Polish plants to be withdrawn from its provisions. The government argued that Poland would comply with the Kyoto Protocol anyway so it did not have to participate in a mechanism aimed at making this compliance easier. However, the European Tribunal stated that participation referred to all countries—also those that planned to comply with the Protocol anyway. According to the Directive, their participation would help other Member States comply. As a result, Polish plants became part of the ETS, too.

Having learned that Polish firms had to comply with the Directive, the government started to work on the initial allocation of permits. A consulting firm called EnergSys had just completed a report on sulphur dioxide emission trading among power plants (see Sect. 8.2). Therefore it was quite obvious that the Ministry of Environment would entrust the same team with the task of preparing the relevant documents concerning carbon dioxide emission. Apart from EnergSys, the consortium included Ecofys (another Polish consulting firm) and Cameron McKenna (an international law firm). The formal transposition of the Directive was completed in 2004 (Polish Official Journal No. 281, item 2784), but work on the initial allocation began the previous year (Jankowski 2007).

The starting point for the allocation work was the total emission of 286.2 million tonnes of CO_2 (CO_2e to be exact), i.e. the Kyoto limit for Poland's large stationary sources. The Commission insisted that this total be reduced to 239.1 million tonnes of CO_2, i.e. by 16.5%. Negotiations started not only regarding this total, but also the way it should be allocated among individual firms. For bureaucratic reasons (mostly on the side of the European Commission), the negotiations were lengthy and concluded as late as in the summer of 2006. Up to that moment Polish firms did not have a chance to participate in European emission trading. Prices were quite attractive then (from €25/t to €30/t). Polish firms were able to start selling when the prices dropped: initially to €15/t, and then almost down to zero.

At the same time, firms from 'old' Member States (EU-15) could participate in trading without any constraints from the outset. But their 'trading' boiled down to borrowing their own permits from the future. On the one hand, this could be applauded as the right decision to predict market prices correctly and to save on 'repaying' what was borrowed. On the other hand, these decisions were probably based on the perception of administrative procedures and the expectation that the Polish allocation plan would not be accepted earlier than in the second half of 2006.

The Polish government tried to allocate the deficit requested by the Commission (16.5%) among individual plants in several ways. There were more than a dozen of such allocations. Power plants were to receive permits for 141.6 million tonnes; the subsequent allocations were 128.4, 126.2, 125.8, 124.9, 125.9, 126.5, 127.0 and—lastly—125.0 million tonnes; their allocation was ultimately cut by 11.1% rather than an average of 16.5%. Thus in relative terms—compared to other Polish emitters—they moved up a bit. Heating plants were to receive 49.7 million tonnes, then subsequently: 39.8, 34.1, 34.4, 36.6, 35.5 and—finally—34.8. In total, their allocation was reduced by 30%, thus—in relative terms—they lost with respect to others.

The non-energy sectors lost as well. The government suggested that steel mills, refineries, lime production, paper mills, sugar mills and cement plants cut their allocations by 16.8%, 21.5%, 27.8%, 24.0%, 27.7% and 18.9%, respectively. As could be anticipated, all of these sectors protested and demanded more favourable treatment. Steel mills retained their relative position (almost). Other sectors received slightly more than was initially planned by the government, but much below what they were aspiring to. The greatest loser was the reserve for newcomers. It would be odd to expect otherwise because there was nobody to protest against bad treatment (Miros and Żylicz 2008).

As a result of participation in the European Trading System, power plant managers started to be sceptical about marketable permits. No traces of enthusiasm could be observed anymore. Also the broader public opinion—favourable towards this instrument earlier because of educational campaigns—has now become sceptical. Part of the scepticism may result from the fact that earlier attempts were addressed at local pollutants (such as sulphur dioxide)—something people understood without any problem. Participation in the European Trading System involves greenhouse gas abatement with carbon dioxide being the most important substance in the GHG group. Carbon dioxide causes global warming which is a phenomenon people in Poland are probably less concerned about, even though—in contrast to some other countries—Poles are not so sceptical about climate change.

References

Atmoterm SA (1996) Report on the project PHARE EC/EPP/91/1.2.2, Opole

Ellerman AD, Büchner BK, Carraro C (eds) (2007) Allocation in the European emissions trading scheme.Rights, rents and fairness. Cambridge University Press. https://cadmus.eui.eu/handle/1814/15699

EnergSys (2003) Opracowanie i wdrożenie systemu zbywalnych uprawnień do emisji w Polsce wraz z wykonaniem analiz kosztów i efektów oraz sformułowaniem uzasadnień dla proponowanych rozwiązań. EnergSys, Warszawa

Jankowski B (2007) Poland. In Ellerman et al (eds) Allocation in the European emissions trading scheme.Rights, rents and fairness, Cambridge University Press, pp 301–337

Marketable Permit Workshop (1996) Proceedings of the Jadwisin conference. Ministry of Environmental Protection, Natural Resources and Forestry

Miros M, Żylicz T (2008) Poland's perspective on EU ETS in 2005–2007. http://www.cdcclimat.com/IMG/pdf/34b-Poland_perspective_EUETS_Miros_Zylicz-2.pdf

MOŚZNiL (1990a) Polityka ekologiczna państwa. Warszawa [State environmental policy]

MOŚZNiL (1990b) Zarys polityki ekologicznej: instrumenty ekonomiczne. Warszawa [Outline of environmental policy: economic instruments]

Stavins RN, Żylicz T (1995) environmental policy in a transition economy: designing tradeable permits for Poland. RFF Discussion Paper, Washington, DC

Żylicz T (1999) Towards tradability of pollution permits in Poland. In Sorrell S, Skea J (eds) Pollution for sale. Emissions trading and joint implementation, Edward Elgar, Cheltenham, pp 124–138

Chapter 9
Air Protection Policy in California

Having discussed the Polish experiments in the previous chapter, we turn our attention to California not only because of its size (it is one of the largest economies in the world), but also because of the fact that its environmental policies are likely to be replicated elsewhere. Moreover, the state has applied marketable permits in areas where this instrument had not been tested before.

California—the most populated state in the USA—is considered one of the most ambitious regions as far as air protection requirements are concerned. This is confirmed not only by state-level activities, but also by federal decisions. For instance, the American Clean Air Act in principle does not allow state jurisdictions to adopt additional state requirements with respect to vehicles registered in their territories. Besides, such requirements are difficult to justify when there are no closed borders between states. California is an exception, because federal regulations allow the state to adopt such requirements (Sect. 9.2), and—moreover—they allow other states to replicate these.

California's administration had to implement certain federal policies analysed in Chap. 6. The following sections discuss policies that were developed at the state level.

9.1 Cap and Trade

Chapter 6 analysed the American system of sulphur dioxide emission trading which led to a drastic decrease in its emission. As a result of this policy, nitrogen oxide emission went down too. At the same time, carbon dioxide (and more generally: GHG) emission did not receive the same priority at the federal level (Schmalensee and Stavins 2019). Some states decided to reduce its emission locally. In the twenty-first century, California established a permit market for GHG emitted by 450 plants responsible for 80% of the total stationary emission in the state (i.e. excluding mobile

T. Żylicz, *Marketable Permits*, SpringerBriefs in Economics,
https://doi.org/10.1007/978-3-032-12133-2_9

sources like cars). The aim is to achieve 60% of the 1990 GHG emission in 2030. Intermediate goals for 2020 were reached faster than planned.

California's programme resembles 'cap and trade', with some substantial modifications. Every year the cap becomes a bit lower (it is reduced by several percentage points). Each source receives (for free) a permit to emit a bit less than it emitted in the previous year. In other words, there is a pool of grandfathered permits. Additional permits can be bought in auction or on the secondary market from those who sell them. To a limited degree (up to 4% of what the plant was grandfathered), large stationary sources can buy emission reduction 'credits' offered by agents who are either not covered by the cap or—as is the case in forestry and agriculture—can capture atmospheric carbon dioxide. Here the system has certain characteristics of the Clean Development Mechanism described in Sect. 5.2, but the absolute level of total emission is more difficult to violate. 'Credits' can be bought from agents registered in the USA only, and officials who confirm the agents' honesty are also responsible for meeting the cap. Creating 'credits' by transferring the emission elsewhere is less likely than in mechanisms applied by the Climate Convention. Of course, cheating is possible, but difficult.

Two instruments are used to enforce these requirements. The penalty for emitting more than permits allow is a multiple of their market price. Consequently, non-compliance (which has actually never happened) may occur as a result of a mistake, not a wilful act. In addition, violating the permits by a unit of emission results in the automatic confiscation of four units from a future period.

In order to reduce the emission from sources not covered by this system directly, a special programme for cars was established. It is discussed in the next section.

9.2 LCFS

The so-called ZEV (*Zero Emission Vehicles*) programme has been promoted since 1990. ZEV emit only water vapour (if they run on hydrogen) or use energy stored in batteries charged by electricity produced in procedures that should be 'clean'. The transition to new technologies is a lengthy process, so since 2011 fuel suppliers have been required to comply with LCFS (*Low Carbon Fuel Standards*) which allow to gradually move towards lower CO_2 emissions. The standards are based on the Life Cycle Analysis of combustion results, especially CO_2, CH_4, N_2O and other GHG. The potential emission (in grammes) is calculated in carbon dioxide equivalents (CO_2e) per every unit of energy of the fuel (i.e. per 1 MJ). It is expected that fuel suppliers will reduce this figure (called *Carbon Index*, CI) by 20% in the twenty-year period between 2010 and 2030.

To avoid the risk of discovering in 2030 that CI was not reduced by 20%, the administration checks every year if it was reduced by one percentage point. A one percentage point reduction in CI every year by each supplier does not make sense from the engineering point of view (see Sect. 3.3). That is why the administration established a market where every year fuel suppliers have to document that an adequate CI was achieved. Those who did more than they were obliged to can sell a part of their effort.

This is not an absolute level system, since compliance is related to the energy content of fuels; when this content increases, CI goes down even if the emission is unchanged. 'Emission trading' is carried out on the state carbon dioxide market described in Sect. 9.1. If the emission attributed to a fuel supplier was higher than the product of the fuel sold and the CI relevant for a given year, the fuel supplier has to buy the missing carbon dioxide permits. If the supplier emitted less, they earn a reduction credit that can be sold.

An additional reason for LCFS being a credit system is the fact that from 2018 on, fuel suppliers can apply to get certificates (to get emission reduction 'credits') if they promote ZEVs—for instance by investing in infrastructure for charging electric cars. The impact of infrastructure investments is regulated separately, and is extremely complicated.

The system is working and has brought about many market changes. For instance, traditional diesel produced out of oil currently makes up less than 50% of the total diesel supply (Bushnell et al. 2023). Having analysed market price trajectories, the administration is contemplating changing the CI reduction target from 20% to 25%, or even to 35% (a reduction by 43% in 2035 can be theoretically justified). In addition to the factors discussed in Sect. 9.1, the popularity of biodiesel (a fuel produced in agriculture) resulted in certificate prices declining from \$200/tCO_2 in 2020–2021 to \$70/tCO_2 in 2024 (California 2024). A decision to make the CI trajectory steeper would cause this price to increase to an earlier high level.

9.3 RPS

Air protection does not confine to trading carbon dioxide emission. Californians expect more activities to eliminate fossil fuels. The acronym RPS stands for *Renewables Portfolio Standard*. This requires all commercial power plants to generate at least 50% of their electricity from renewable sources by 2030. To this end, electricity producers apply for certificates to confirm renewability. In order to be recognised as renewable, the electricity should be generated from one of the 17 sources (such as biodiesel, sea tides, wind etc.) identified in the relevant regulations (Green and Crume 2017). The RPS is to approach 50% gradually.

The list of legitimate renewable sources is extensive, but keeps shrinking. For instance, new applications from some hydroelectric generation units and from some municipal solid waste incinerators have not been accepted since 2013 and 2016, respectively. Even before eligibility was constrained, requirements were adopted to eliminate sources whose renewability was doubtful. Applicants have to describe the technology applied to demonstrate its viability. Administrators see environmental protection and sustainable development as priorities, but the marketability of permits seems to be an obvious solution as well.

In order not to force power plants to have their RPS index grow at a uniform rate every year, its surpluses and deficits can be traded. If a power plant achieved a higher index for a given year it can sell its surplus to one with a deficit. The system is highly complicated since it has to take into account the specific requirements of the electricity market, including the need to meet the demand and supply in every moment.

References

Bushnell J, Lade G, Smith A, Witcover J, Xiao W (2023) Forecasting credit supply demand balance for the low-carbon fuel standard program. Working Paper, Energy Institute at Haas, University of California, Berkeley (WP–340) https://haas.berkeley.edu/energy-institute/research/abstracts/wp-340/

California Air Resources Board (2024) Cap-and-trade program data dashboard. https://ww2.arb.ca.gov/our-work/programs/cap-and-trade-program/program-data/cap-and-trade-program-data-dashboard#Figure7

Green L, Crume C (2017) Renewables portfolio standard eligibility guidebook. 9th edn. California Energy Commission. Publication Number: CEC-300-2016-006-ED9-CMFREV

Schmalensee R, Stavins RN (2019) Policy evolution under the Clean Air Act. J Econ Persp 33 (4):27–50. https://www.aeaweb.org/articles?id=10.1257/jep.33.4.27

Chapter 10
Other Applications of Marketable Permits

10.1 Marketable Harvest Quotas

Fisheries constitute a specialized sector within the economy. In a country like Poland, their importance is not very high. For some regions, however, they can be very important from the point of view of labour and food markets. As far as aquifers are concerned, fishery management can be an important factor determining the resilience of ecosystems.

At the turn of the twentieth century, marketable harvest quotas became quite popular in many regions of the world (Chu 2009). Some analysts (e.g. (Sterner 2003)) consider them as important as marketable pollution permits. The mechanism establishes a *Total Allowable Catch* (TAC) for a given aquifer, allocates it among fishermen or fishing firms, and allows transfers. As for marketable pollution permits analysed in previous chapters, the initial allocation is determined by grandfathering or by an auction. This instrument made it possible to replace or enhance alternative methods of fishery management, such as protection periods which sometimes extended over 360 days in a year, resulting in socially inefficient investment levels: fishing firms kept their vessels ready all year round to make revenues in just a few days.

Not all fishery-related problems are solved with marketable harvest quotas. The mechanism may lead to so-called *highgrading*, i.e. getting rid of fish caught (often already dead) that fishermen do not want subtracted from the harvesting limit. As a result, the official harvest includes only the catch that contributes to revenue maximisation, but actual harvests are higher than allowed by authorities. Nevertheless—when all advantages and disadvantages are taken into consideration—the bottom line is that marketable harvest quotas improve the effectiveness of protecting marine ecosystems (Mackenzie 2008). By the way, highgrading is a problem that exists irrespective of whether quotas are marketable or not.

T. Żylicz, *Marketable Permits*, SpringerBriefs in Economics,
https://doi.org/10.1007/978-3-032-12133-2_10

Applying marketable permits in fishery management turned out to be more complicated than expected. The idea of setting TACs for an aquifer ignores the complicated relationships between the species that populate it and are of economic interest. Sophisticated mathematical models (Conrad and Rondeau 2020) demonstrate that there is no simple rule for how to determine the scale that is to be allocated between potential users. Squires and Walden (2022) explain that an efficient allocation may depend on a number of circumstances, such as interactions with other species as well as the economic characteristics of fishing fleets. For instance, Grafton et al. (2000) documented that allowing fishermen to transfer allocations actually reduced efficiency, as shown by the case of the Canadian Pacific halibut. By the way, Schnier and Felthoven (2013) found that fishing fleet inefficiency contributed significantly to the introduction of quota transferability. Biologists and other natural scientists (e.g. (Valdovinos et al. 2024), (Kushal et al. 2024)) explain that the trophic connections between exploited organisms are so complex that it is almost impossible to establish a cap for a given species that could be split among potential users without an administrative control.

Limiting harvests is necessary even with respect to species that seem to be very common. Perhaps it comes as a surprise that the North Sea herring was close to extinction in the 1970s. Only banning harvests—enforced by the European Union—saved its population (Bjørndal and Conrad 1987). The ban was lifted when the herring population started to show appropriate vitality.

Protection against excessive harvests is particularly essential in the case of lakes and semi-enclosed seas such as the Baltic Sea. Since 1973 its marine resources have been protected by the Gdansk Convention which established a secretariate in Gdansk authorised with setting and allocating harvest quotas. After 2004, when the Baltic Sea became an internal aquifer of the European Union almost entirely, the European Council assumed responsibility and has been deciding on harvest quotas for member states. Quotas are based on the assessment made by ICES (*International Council for the Exploration of the Sea*). Its goal is to study marine ecosystems and the services they provide, and to use this knowledge to achieve conservation, management and sustainability objectives. However, the harvest quotas established by the European Council are also motivated by political considerations.

The European Council decides on TACs for the five most important Baltic species: cod, herring, sprat, salmon and flounder (or plaice, to be exact). Other species can be harvested too, but their commercial importance is lower. In 2024 the sum of allowed catches was: 78,383 t for herring, 935 t for cod, 201,000 t for sprat, 53,967 t for salmon and 11,313 t for flounder (MRiRW 2023). In every case these numbers were much lower than before due to the seriously endangered populations of some species, above all cod. Cod harvests decreased drastically: in 1983–2013 they were reduced by a factor of ten (Nieminen & Grønbak Nieminen and Grønbæk 2016), and subsequently even more. There is a *de facto* moratorium on catching cod and salmon as they may be harvested only as by-catch (if they are found in a net cast with the purpose of catching something else).

The quotas allocated by the European Council are not really tradable. Theoretically, the Council accepts their marketability, but allocations are low and no country is brave enough to assume the role of seller, since the government would have to admit that—contrary to what it claimed in the negotiation process—it was not going to use the entire allocation. National regulations allow transfers of individual species. In Poland this is sometimes a 1:1 exchange (e.g. 1 kg of herring for 1 kg of sprat), but not always. For instance, 1 kg of rosefish can be exchanged for 2 kg of mackerel, or 1 piece of salmon for 40 kg of cod. Transfers can take place between fishermen registered in different countries. Nevertheless they are rarely carried out.

10.2 Water Withdrawals

Water withdrawals are regulated by marketable permits in several areas. Two of these are of particular interest due to the very difficult problems that needed solving. Lake Mead in the USA and the Murray-Darling basin in Australia will be analysed here. The first is a remarkable attempt to solve an environmental problem with serious transboundary implications. The second one addresses an environmental problem while paying particular attention to economic and social issues.

In the 1930s, a gigantic dam was constructed on the Colorado river. It created a retention reservoir—called Lake Mead—at the border of Arizona and Nevada (hundreds of kilometres from the Mexican border) with a volume of 32 km^3.

As agreed in a bilateral treaty of 1944, Americans committed themselves to leave at least 28 km^3 per year reaching the Mexican border along the Colorado river (around 10% of its annual flow; the rest is used mainly in US irrigation systems). Americans complied with their commitment but Mexicans complained about water quality. The lower parts of the Colorado river were so salty that the water could not be used even for agricultural purposes (not to mention municipal purposes). Mexicans demanded that the quality of the water reaching their border be improved (the water becomes increasingly salty as it flows through the agricultural irrigation systems). In 2012 the US agreed that the guaranteed amount of water would be available in Lake Mead.

In other words, Mexicans received the property right to water stored not on their territory but in the USA. In particular, they can sell their rights to American agents. In fact, the ownership structure is somewhat more complicated, because indigenous people (Native Americans) insist that they have been discriminated and should be given more rights to the river. Still, Lake Mead is an example of a solution based on marketable permits for water.

This is not an absolute limit system because the amount of water that may be withdrawn is subject to meteorological conditions. The permits specify not absolute quantities, but shares. The initial allocation between Americans and Mexicans resulted from a political decision. The allocation between Americans is based mainly on a 'grandfather principle' but takes additional factors into account since the volume of water stored is variable. In wet years, the elevation of the water surface is 375 m above sea level. A record low level of 328 m was documented in 2022. The right to withdraw water depends on this figure in a very complex way.

Australia has a long history of attempting to make water withdrawals marketable. The first possibility was introduced by the Natural Resources Management Act of 2004. In 2009, amendments were adopted to separate or 'unbundle' water rights in the watersheds of two major Australian rivers: Murray and Darling. When water rights are 'unbundled', they become separate from a specific location and this enables transfers or at least makes them easier. In 2019 these regulations were incorporated in the Landscape South Australia Act. In 2022 the Minister for the Environment and Water presented the final roadmap report, and in 2023 the Water Amendment ('Restoring Our Rivers') Act was adopted. It addressed problems found by the Australian Competition and Consumer Commission (ACCC) that had been published in 2021 (ACCC 2021).

The market performed well but several problems were identified. Some of the issues—e.g. promoting competition and eliminating information asymmetry—are common for all markets. Still, some students may be puzzled by the arguments of citizens for 'bundling' rights, i.e. making them non-marketable again, which were presented in the report. This problem is similar to the one mentioned in the Sect. (10.1) in the context of harvest quotas. Marketability promotes efficiency. However, profit maximisation is not the sole criterion for economic activities. The so-called Prime Nations, i.e. people who lived in Australia before it became a British colony, emphasise that water consumption—similarly to the use of other natural resources—should serve social needs and not profit maximisation.

Additional problems arise from the fact that many jurisdictions—both federal and state—must cooperate in the course of implementing basin-wide policies.

Nevertheless the overall assessment is positive. The Australian government indicates that agricultural production from irrigated land in the basin (where farmers have been the major end users of the water) has grown despite bad and volatile climatic conditions. The benefits are not confined to transferring water to where it is most valuable. Agricultural economists have demonstrated that selling water surpluses provides capital that allows to switch to newer farming technologies. This incentivises economic agents to use less water.

10.3 Transferable Development Rights

Every country has legislation aimed at protecting the landscape. In some areas the legislation does not allow the construction of high buildings. Owners of real estate who cannot invest in a high building ask authorities for compensation. This leads to disagreements, because the authorities are interested in paying as little as possible and argue that building additional floors would not be very profitable. Meanwhile the owners claim huge losses from not having these additional floors.

Transferable development rights—which have not been used very frequently—can solve the problem. The idea is to issue rights that are not sufficient to construct a high building even in a non-protected area. Let us assume that every real estate owner gets the right to construct a 3-storey building. Landscape protection laws allow even higher buildings to be constructed in non-protected areas. The construction of a 7-storey building would require obtaining permits for 4 additional floors. Would there be a supply of such permits? The obvious candidates for sellers are the owners of lots located in protected areas. If the legislation allows only 2-storey buildings in these areas, each owner has an unused permit for 1 floor. Four such owners (jointly) have permits that are required by the buyer. Of course, the assumption of three storeys was given merely as an example. In practice, this number depends on the conditions specific for a given region.

The system described above is superior to the traditional solution, because it frees authorities from negotiating the level of compensations. If the local economy is developing dynamically, the demand for constructing tall buildings is high, so the price offered for an additional storey must be high. If the local economy is stagnating, the demand for tall buildings is weak; real estate owners located in protected areas cannot argue that they are losing large sums of money by being deprived of the possibility to construct tall buildings, because they get exactly what those who construct tall buildings are willing to pay.

This mechanism has not been widespread, but in Chicago and New York it was applied, among other things, to protect fragments of cities that are valuable because of their historical heritage. It had dozens of applications in the United States, despite doubts if it was consistent with the Constitution (more specifically with the Fifth Amendment, the so called 'Takings' Clause of 1789–1791: 'nor shall private property be taken for public use, without just compensation') which places certain limits on regulations of this type (Miller 1999). The main advantage of the mechanism is letting the market rather than the government determine the compensation and this is exactly what the Amendment deals with.

It can also be applied to constrain the economic use of biodiversity-rich habitats. In this case, too, real estate owners who are affected by environmental regulations ask for financial compensations. Cumbersome negotiations can be avoided by imposing some constraints universally and letting real estate owners located in non-protected areas buy permits from those who cannot use them in situ (Panayotou 1994).

Similarly, the water balance may be improved by putting constraints on the amount of surface covered with concrete. The essence of transferable development rights is to create a demand for certain goods while making sure that their supply will exist as well. As usually, those who own lots located in protected areas can expect constraints resulting from protection to be compensated. Yet instead of involving the state budget and exposing government officials to inconvenient negotiations, compensations can be left to market forces.

Transferable development rights are consistent with Herman Daly's recommendation to separate scale and allocation (see Sect. 2.2). The scale, i.e. determining the limits to interference in the environment, is to be decided by the administration.

The allocation, i.e. determining who will use what is available for use, should be left to market forces since the market knows better than officials how to use resources most efficiently.

10.4 Tradable Packaging Waste Recovery Notes

In United Kingdom a unique instrument was introduced to encourage cost-effective improvements in packaging waste management (Sterner 2003, pp. 371–372). It was prompted by the EU Packaging and Packaging Waste Directive (94/62). The Directive introduced some obvious obligations (to be fulfilled by member states) aimed at reducing the toxicity of packaging materials. It also introduced certain quantified targets for reuse and recycling that were to be reached by certain dates.

While transposing the Directive, the UK government assumed correctly that all agents in a value chain that culminates in the sale of an end product have certain roles in its packaging. Hence in 1997 it introduced Producers Responsibility Obligation Regulations, addressing four stages: (1) the production of raw materials, (2) turning the raw materials into packaging, (3) placing goods into or filling packaging, and (4) retail. The responsibility 'shares' assigned to each stage may vary by year and product type. The shares are between 0% and 100%; late stages are the most responsible for the problem of course, but all have some responsibility. The numbers are determined by administrators, but are known to all of the agents who are obliged to submit an appropriate quantity of reuse/recycle obligation notes.

However, the agents do not need to be physically involved in reuse/recycle activities. They can finance relevant activities undertaken by someone else. Therefore, these obligations—called Packaging Recovery Notes—are tradable. The instrument proved to be successful, so the regulations have been continued even after Brexit (The Environment Exchange 2024).

10.5 Saving the Climate

Contemporary climatology leaves no doubt that the observed temperature rise has been caused by the emission of carbon dioxide (and other GHG) by the world economy. In 1992–2022, since the signing of the Climate Convention, this emission grew almost twofold: from around 25 billion tonnes per year to around 48 billion tonnes. Exact figures cannot be quoted, since non-Annex I countries do not have a reporting obligation. Emission estimates are based on the available economic statistics (Statista 2024b).

Annex I contribution (see Sects. 5.2 and 7.1) is small and steadily decreasing, but the climate will not be saved even if Annex I countries reduce their emission to zero. It is necessary to reduce global emission, not the emission from just one region. There are several ideas how to do this, one of which is based on the concept of marketable permits. The global population is close to 8 billion. The average annual emission per capita is thus around 6 tonnes of CO_2. Let us agree that a country with population L can emit 6L tonnes (has 6L permits). If the actual per capita emission is higher than 6 tonnes, missing permits must be bought, and if the actual per capita emission is lower, not all permits are used and their surplus can be sold.

In European countries, the average per capita emission originating from burning fossil fuels (its main source) is higher than 6 tonnes (e.g. 7.62 t in Norway, 8.15 t in Germany, 8.53 t in Poland, 9.55 t in the Czech Republic). It is also higher in many other wealthy countries: 8.61 t in Japan, 14.44 t in the USA, 15.22 t in Canada. Likewise, it is higher in China which—since 2004—has been the largest carbon dioxide emitter in the world with 8.55 t per capita. In contrast, in countries that are less developed economically it is usually much lower: 0.07 t in Burundi, 0.14 t in Afghanistan, 0.29 t in Mozambique, 0.63 t in Bangladesh, 1.08 t in Guatemala, 1.85 t in Bolivia, 1.98 t in India, 2.96 t in Tunisia, 3.27 t in Vietnam, 4.03 t in Romania, etc. (European Commission 2024c).

The per capita cap can be gradually decreased from the initial 6 t, according to climatologists' recommendations. The marketability of permits proportional to the population would imply money transfers from wealthy countries to poor ones, consistently with what has usually been postulated.

In order to get an idea of the money transfers implied by this mechanism, it may be estimated that the USA would record a 'deficit' of permits equal to 8.44 tonnes per capita, i.e. 2,870 million tonnes. At the same time, India would record a 'surplus' of permits equal to 4.02 tonnes per capita, i.e. 5,745 million tonnes. It is difficult to predict the price of a permit. Surely it would be much lower than that observed in the ETS (Sect. 7.3). If one agrees (with Nordhaus 2007) that the price of $10/t$CO_2$ is justified, the USA would have to spend USD 28 billion on additional permits, and India could count on revenues of USD 57 billion. These figures are not far from the flows that have lately been observed. In 2023, the US government spent more—over USD 60 billion—on development assistance for the world (OECD 2024). The GDP of India in 2022 was USD 3,417 billion (World Bank 2024), so the hypothetical revenues from selling permits would amount to less than 2% of its GDP.

A solution is needed for wealthy countries like Switzerland which currently emit below 6 tonnes (4.11 tonnes) and so are sellers (not buyers) of permits. Similarly, less developed countries that emit a lot (in Kazakhstan the current emission is 12.85 tonnes) and are therefore potential buyers also require a solution, because it is generally expected that money should flow in the opposite direction (from Switzerland to Kazakhstan). However, if the cap goes down sufficiently quickly then even wealthy countries with relatively low current emission will have to buy missing permits in the future.

The marketable permit system outlined above could help save the climate, and simultaneously trigger money flows to economies that need them most. The idea was presented many years ago (Żylicz 2010). It is being repeated from time to time but has never gained any political support. Wealthy countries do not wish to have an allocation that is proportional to the population, arguing that the allocation of permits should reflect material welfare as well. This ideology implies that higher GDP per capita should result in higher emission per capita. There are also other arguments against allocation based on uniform per capita emission (Pettersson et al. 2014). These refer to the fact that countries may differ in geographical conditions, e.g. being exposed to different meteorological conditions such as mean temperature.

References

Australian Competition & Consumer Commission (ACCC) (2021) Murray–Darling Basin water markets inquiry. Final report. Canberra

Bjørndal T, Conrad J (1987) The dynamics of open access fishery. Can J Econ 20(1):74–85. https://econpapers.repec.org/article/cjeissued/v_3a20_3ay_3a1987_3ai_3a1_3ap_3a74-85.htm

Chu C (2009) Thirty years later: the global growth of ITQs and their influence on stock status in marine fisheries. Fish Fish 10(2):217–230. https://onlinelibrary.wiley.com/doi/10.1111/j.1467-2979.2008.00313.x

Conrad JM, Rondeau D (2020) Natural resource economics: analysis, theory, and applications. Cambridge University Press, Cambridge

European Commission (2024c) GHG emissions of all world countries. https://edgar.jrc.ec.europa.eu/report_2023#emissions_table

Grafton RQ, Squires D, Fox KJ (2000) Private property and economic efficiency: a study of a common-pool resource. J Law Econ 43(2):679–714

Kushal A, Springborn M, Valdovinos F (2024) Assessing impacts of bycatch policies and fishers' heterogeneous information on food webs and fishery sustainability. Philos Trans R Soc B 379:20230181. https://doi.org/10.1098/rstb.2023.0181

Mackenzie D (2008) Shares' in fish stocks halt commercial free-for-all. New Scientist, 18 Sept. https://www.newscientist.com/article/dn14762-shares-in-fish-stocks-halt-commercial-free-for-all/

Miller AJ (1999) Transferable development rights in the constitutional landscape: has Penn Central failed to weather the storm? Nat Resour J 39(3):459–516. https://digitalrepository.unm.edu/nrj/vol39/iss3/3

MRiRW (2023) Notatka o porozumieniu w sprawie połowów bałtyckich w 2024 r. https://www.gov.pl/web/agriculture/a-political-agreement-was-reached-on-the-fishing-opportunities-in-the-baltic-sea

Nieminen E, Grønbæk L (2016) International agreements in the multispecies Baltic Sea Fisheries. Environ Resour Econ 65(1):109–134

Nordhaus WD (2007) A review of the Stern Review on the economics of climate change. J Econ Lit 45(3):686–702. https://www.aeaweb.org/articles?id=10.1257/jel.45.3.686

OECD (2024) Official development assistance. https://www.oecd.org/dac/financing-sustainable-development/development-finance-standards/official-development-assistance.htm

Panayotou T (1994) Conservation of biodiversity and economic development: the concept of transferable development rights. Environ Resour Econ 4(1):95–110. https://econpapers.repec.org/article/kapenreec/v_3a4_3ay_3a1994_3ai_3a1_3ap_3a91-110.htm

Pettersson F, Maddison D, Acar S, Söderholm P (2014) Convergence of carbon dioxide emissions: a review of the literature. Int Rev Environ Resour Econ 7(2):141–178. http://dx.doi.org/10.1561/101.00000059

Schnier KE, Felthoven RG (2013) Production efficiency and exit in rights-based fisheries. Land Econ 89(3):538–557

Squires D, Walden J (2022) The economics of production in marine fisheries. In Ray SC, Chambers RG, Kumbhakar SC (eds) Handbook of production economics. Springer, pp 1339–1378

Statista (2024b) Carbon dioxide emissions of the most polluting countries worldwide in 2010 and 2023. https://www.statista.com/statistics/270499/co2-emissions-in-selected-countries/

Sterner T (2003) Policy instrument for environmental and natural resource management. Resources for the Future Press, Washington, DC. https://nguyenduyliemgis.wordpress.com/wp-content/uploads/2015/01/policy-instruments-for-environmental-and-natural-resource-management-google-book.pdf

The Environment Exchange (t2e) (2024) Packaging recovery notes. https://www.t2e.co.uk/markets/packaging-recovery-notes

Valdovinos F, Bodini A, Jordán F (2024) Connected interactions: enriching food web research by spatial and social interactions. Philos Trans R Soc B 379:20230163. https://doi.org/10.1098/rstb.2023.0163

World Bank (2024) GDP tables. https://data.worldbank.org/indicator/NY.GDP.MKTP.CD

Żylicz T (2010) Goals and principles of environmental policy. Int Rev Environ Resour Econ 3(4):299–334. http://dx.doi.org/10.1561/101.00000028

Chapter 11
Postscript

Since the publication of Martin Weitzman's famous paper (1974) which compared price—and quantity-based instruments, economists have been deliberating when marketable permits (a quantity instrument) are better than Pigouvian taxes (a price instrument). Theoretically, these are equivalent. However, Weitzman noted that this equivalence is true in a world of perfect information only: in a world where all agents are perfectly informed about anything they do. There is no such comfort in environmental protection policy. When deciding on a cap or on a Pigouvian tax rate, authorities can err and miscalculate the costs and benefits affecting the interested parties, i.e. firms and their neighbourhoods.

The so-called Weitzman rule (see e.g. (Sterner 2003, pp. 150–152)) indicates that in certain circumstances permits are more reliable than Pigouvian taxes, but in other circumstances it is the other way around. Yet, unlike Pigouvian taxes, marketable permits attach priority to nature, not to the economy. Besides, they separate scale and allocation decisions clearly. There is one more advantage of this instrument, especially in the context of international climate protection. The establishment of caps for emission implies a lower risk of fraud than in the case of taxation which—theoretically—allows to achieve the same effect. This is because tax revenues can be used to indirectly subsidise emitters that were supposed to be disciplined by the tax. This is an important reason why the European Commission is afraid that exporters of products subject to CBAM may claim having paid higher carbon taxes than they have in reality, when indirect subsidies are taken into account.

A recent review of instruments applied to protect the global climate (Wood Mackenzie 2024), which cover around 25% of the global emission, indicated that there were both tax systems and marketable permit schemes. The latter—like the ETS—cover more emissions than tax systems. The Weitzman rule suggests that it should be the other way around. The prominent position of marketable permits may probably be explained by the desire to implement instruments that are more fraud-proof.

T. Żylicz, *Marketable Permits*, SpringerBriefs in Economics,
https://doi.org/10.1007/978-3-032-12133-2_11

The application of marketable permits for carbon dioxide emission—whether in Europe or in China—is justified by the fact that its release to the atmosphere does not have localised effects but affects the global climate. Therefore any source can be seen as a potential substitute for any other one. From the point of view of climate protection, it does not make any difference where the emission takes place.

The widespread application of marketable permits for the emission of carbon dioxide is not always correlated with sincere and effective attempts to save the climate. Such attempts require establishing a cap for emission. Experience from many systems shows that the formal existence of a cap does not necessarily guarantee success. In the Chinese system, which many expect to bring significant improvements, the cap is almost 4 billion tonnes, i.e. more than in the ETS (but less than 40% of the country's emission estimated at 11 billion tonnes). However, the emission can easily 'leak' from where it is capped. Indeed, a permit price that is equivalent to several dollars per tonne suggests that no sincere effort to protect the climate is being made. Chinese requirements are not very demanding, but even a market as problematic as this one provides incentives to seek technologies that result in lower emission. Hence the Chinese carbon policy requires special attention and should not be downplayed.

Global applications of marketable permits do not confine to carbon dioxide emission. The instrument has been successfully implemented in other areas too. There is no doubt that permits can be applied to reduce the emission of other pollutants as well. In the USA, marketable permits contributed to the success of combating 'acid rain' and smog. In Poland, the Chorzów experiment proved that local air quality could be improved quickly and at a relatively low cost by reducing the emission of many 'traditional' pollutants in a flexible way.

Marketable permits are considered an 'American' instrument and indeed they were invented on the western side of the Atlantic Ocean. The earliest implementations were carried out in the USA. For many years, marketable permits were approached with distrust in Europe. Thanks to the establishment of the ETS, marketable permits started to be considered a standard instrument of environmental policy everywhere, including in Europe, but only as late as in the twenty-first century. Given the numerous textbook mistakes made in the implementation phase of ETS (manipulating with initial allocation when trading was already allowed, coexistence with subsidies, etc.), some sceptics say that these mistakes were made on purpose, to disrepute this overseas invention. Nevertheless it cannot be considered an American novelty anymore. China has announced proudly that the country has the largest carbon dioxide emission trading system in the world (Stavins 2018). As argued above, this is an exaggeration: although it does cover more emission than in Europe, the system is so soft that the permit price is a dozen times lower than in Europe.

Marketable permits are often linked to pollution, but their applications in the world are much broader. In many places they address fishery problems. The earliest applications of marketable harvest quotas were carried out in Canada and New Zealand. Presently they can be found in many regions including the Baltic Sea (albeit at a low scale). In the case of Lake Mead and the Murray-Darling basin, marketable water rights are applied. Meanwhile California's environmental policy promotes markets for LCFS and RPS. These were introduced as air protection measures but serve other purposes as well.

Marketable permits have become popular all over the world. It is ironic that American populists who enjoy surprisingly high social support are trying to discredit the permits by substituting 'cap and trade' with the goofy expression of 'cap and tax'. This does not make much sense, but may be catchy for non-professionals.

Irrespective of some strange developments, marketable permits have become a standard environmental policy instrument. They free the administration from the burden of studying the unique circumstances of individual firms. They allow to concentrate on what is essential from the point of view of environmental protection. At the same time—by establishing an initial allocation—they can support any distribution of economic burdens. Grandfathered allocations (especially when granted for free) are an important condition of the political feasibility of the instrument.

In the short run, marketable permits are sometimes seen as not very satisfactory since the scale of environmental protection is determined by a cap and the reduction of the negative impact is not guaranteed. In the long run, however—as a result of minimising the cost of reaching the cap—marketable permits demonstrate that environmental protection is less expensive than might be expected. This encourages adopting more ambitious goals in the future.

An important point of criticism is linked to the discussion of 'financialisation of nature' (Smith 2021). The word 'financialisation' refers to the tendency to treat everything as a financial asset. One of the reasons for the crisis that erupted in 2008 was the sale of assets whose value was poorly understood because they did not correspond to anything tangible; people were buying and selling so-called derivatives, i.e. elements of contracts to buy or sell something in the future. The contracts were subject to uncertainty, and in fact this was the commodity that people tried to attach some price to.

Financial markets gained bad reputation, which was extrapolated to marketable permits. These are seen as an attempt to put a price on everything—including nature. It is true that many offsetting programmes are highly controversial. The controversies are associated with two different aspects of offsetting. One is linked to geographical distance while the other to 'diluting a cap'. Critics point out the fact that certain damage incurred in one location cannot be compensated by carrying out improvements elsewhere. Biodiversity protection serves as an example of this sort of misunderstanding; restoring a habitat in one place may not be sufficient to compensate for its loss somewhere else. A 'credit' resulting from a project carried out under a different jurisdiction than the one that established a cap for some environmental damage *de facto* lowers the cap. In the case of environmental damage that is not sensitive to where the emission takes place (as is the case with climate-affecting emission of GHG), relaxing the cap in one location can indeed be compensated by lower emission elsewhere. But otherwise (as is the case with 'acid rain' or smog) compensations are more difficult to justify.

Climate change is an interesting example of controversies related to crediting. Article 12 of the Kyoto Protocol introduced the Clean Development Mechanism (CDM) in order to let non-Annex I countries undertake decarbonization projects. A lot of such projects received 'credits' (in terms of carbon dioxide emission reduced) that—in principle—can be purchased by firms from Annex I countries which are supposed to hold sufficient numbers of permits. The problem is that Annex I firms are bound by rigorous caps (in the European Union they participate in the ETS), while firms willing to sell 'credits' acquired in CDM procedures are not bound by any caps. In order to protect their caps from being *de facto* lowered by CDM 'credits', Annex I jurisdictions impose certain limits on the number of 'alien' permits that may be recognized. For instance, CDM 'credits' acquired after 2012 are not accepted in the ETS at all. In California's systems some 'credits' are allowed, but they must be issued by US authorities.

The criticism related to financialisation is being brought up even in systems bound by stringent caps, without any offsetting opportunities. Some environmental activists do not wish to see any economic arguments in the context of nature protection. They expect nature to be esteemed irrespective of the costs incurred; they would like to see a world where people respect all natural resources and are not guided by commercial profit considerations. Such a world would indeed be totally different, but it is questionable whether societies will choose such an option within the foreseeable future.

Assuming that people are not likely to abandon their preference for the kind of welfare that they aspire to, environmental protection should be enforced by authorities. Thus some sort of permits are necessary. Of course, these can be non-tradeable, but there are many good reasons to make them marketable.

Despite the advantages of marketable permits, several problems need to be solved to make sure that their application serves economic and public purposes well. It must be emphasised that marketable permits are to improve economic efficiency rather than environmental quality. They simply help to achieve environmental objectives determined by society at the least cost. Of course, in the long run, if these objectives turn out not to be as expensive as people were fearing, marketable permits may encourage setting more ambitious targets, but this is not their primary role.

At the same time, societies expect subsidies to result in improved environmental quality. In the presence of marketable permits (as explained in Sect. 2.6), subsidies do not result in the expected improvements, and people are disappointed. As environmental subsidies are likely to be continued, modalities need to be worked out so that these two instruments can co-exist. Otherwise the advantages of marketable permits may be perceived as too low to justify their implementation.

The advantages of cap-and-trade systems justify their introduction wherever authorities are able to enforce a limit for some sort of environmental use. The problem is that in numerous cases there is no such authority. Climate protection that calls for introducing a global 'cap' for carbon dioxide emission serves as the best example. There is a universal convention (*Framework Convention on Climate Change* of 1992), but the 'cap' does not exist since countries are sovereign and there is no authority to enforce it.

At the same time, some regions—e.g. the European Union—have 'caps' that can be enforced. There is a temptation to create 'credits' to subtract from some 'cap', i.e. to create 'credits' which can be purchased by agents who otherwise would have to buy a part of the 'cap'. The problem is, however, that such 'credits' *de facto* increase the 'cap', contrary to what was its *raison d'être*. Consequently, the authorities that administer the 'caps' and feel responsible for their enforcement are reluctant to allow the use of 'credits'. California has a principle that 'credits' bought from agents not covered by the state-wide 'cap' cannot exceed 4% of the initial allocation. Additionally, 'credits' can be bought from agents registered in the USA only. In ETS, 'credits' obtained through the CDM have not been allowed at all since 2012.

Yet 'credit' systems are contemplated in many areas (e.g. climate or biodiversity protection), so there needs to be a way to couple them with 'cap' systems. An obvious requirement for the coexistence of the two would be to make sure that 'credits' are calculated with respect to a well-defined and meaningful baseline. The baseline should be common and binding for every agent not covered by the 'cap'. This, however, is equivalent to extending the 'cap' to all agents, which was assumed impossible in the first place. Hence the challenge is to create a fraud-proof 'credit' system where an overall 'cap' cannot be enforced.

Another problem surfaced when detailed studies of fisheries were carried out. It turned out that the concept of TAC with respect to a single species is difficult to quantify. Ecological relationships are so complex that transferring a right to harvest a particular species from one fisher to another (who has a right to harvest some other species too) may compromise the sustainability of habitats. In other words, the catches of various species influence one another. When designing a permit market, policymakers should take into account the non-linear (synergistic) effects.

The problem is not new (see Sect. 2.5). Nevertheless, all actual applications assume that the various objectives addressed by policymakers (such as the reduction of various pollutants or the allowable catches of various species) interact with each other linearly. In order to cope with more complex relationships, policymakers should go beyond the classic Montgomery model (see Sect. 2.1). Perhaps some additional research (as mentioned in 2.5) along these lines would be justified.

It has been emphasised that marketable permits help to arrive at least-cost solutions. They improve the economic efficiency of achieving environmental policy objectives. Yet economic efficiency is not the only matter of concern. In particular, people care for the integrity of ecosystems and for social fairness. It was just observed above that regulating synergistic pollutants or making harvest quota transferable requires more complex policies. The Murray basin experience indicates that marketable water withdrawals may compromise social fairness expectations. A study commissioned by the Australian government confirmed that making water withdrawals marketable improved efficiency and—on average—served economic development. At the same time, losers called for the 're-bundling' of water rights with land ownership, that is for making these rights non-marketable.

The controversial outcomes of some applications show that improved efficiency may be accompanied by disturbing social consequences. Both Australian and American (Lake Mead) experiences demonstrate that not everyone benefits equally, and moreover economic efficiency does not appeal to some ethnic groups whose views should also be taken into account by policymakers. Early concerns about the unwanted economic consequences of marketable permits—such as the strategic behaviour of big companies, and monopolisation—proved premature. Perhaps the very careful design of permit markets prevented adverse effects of this kind.

Analyses of marketable permits reveal concerns about the 'financialisation' of nature. Some people claim that nature is priceless and should not be traded. They do not object to non-marketable permits, since human activities do require using nature. However, if an economic agent uses less than the permit allows, then the unused part of the permit should be confiscated rather than sold. This philosophy assumes that permits are granted according to the perfect knowledge of the granting authority. If a permit is found to be excessive, it means that somebody miscalculated something. This philosophy neglects a number of real world issues such as market dynamics, technological progress, asymmetric information, and so on.

Even though there are many good reasons for making permits marketable, concerns regarding 'finacialisation' should not be downplayed. Indeed there are people who see nature as something that should not be treated as a commodity and the marketability of permits is not consistent with their worldview. Instead of being ridiculed, this worldview should be taken into account, and the ecological consequences of alternative policies have to be scrutinised. If the marketability of permits yields results that are worse than administrative decisions, authorities should modify their policies.

References

Smith T (2021) Financialisation of nature. Vienna university of economics and business, Discussion Paper 08/2021. https://www.academia.edu/115823533/Financialisation_of_Nature

Stavins RN (2018) What should we make of China's announcement of a national CO2 trading system. https://www.robertstavinsblog.org/2018/01/

Sterner T (2003) Policy instrument for environmental and natural resource management. Resources for the future press, Washington, DC. https://nguyenduyliemgis.wordpress.com/wp-content/uploads/2015/01/policy-instruments-for-environmental-and-natural-resource-management-google-book.pdf

Weitzman M (1974) Prices vs. quantities. Rev Econ Stud 41(4):477–491. https://scholar.harvard.edu/weitzman/files/prices_vs_quantities.pdf

Wood Mackenzie (2024) Carbon markets: 5 things to look for in 2024. https://www.woodmac.com/news/opinion/carbon-markets-2024-outlook/

Multiple Choice Test Questions

1. Cost-effectiveness in environmental policy means that

   [a] abatement costs should be consistent with accounting regulations
   [b] the policy is adopted by a democratically elected government
   [c] the policy is approved in a democratic procedure
   [d] environmental protection is understood in a holistic way (nature cannot be separated into air, water and soil components)
   [e] **none of these**

2. The Fox River experiment

   [a] allowed agricultural pollution caused by excessive fertiliser application to be compensated by more effective municipal sewage treatment
   [b] **allowed higher discharges from paper mills to be compensated by lower discharges from municipal sewage treatment plants (or vice versa)**
   [c] allowed higher current discharges to be compensated by lower discharges in the future
   [d] required discharges from paper mills to be justified by the production sold
   [e] none of these

3. Auctions of marketable permits

   [a] provide a good platform for selling emission reduction 'credits'
   [b] provide an opportunity for firms that undertake abatement projects to sell the results of their emission reduction
   [c] **are organised by environmental protection authorities**
   [d] provide an opportunity to change the cap (maximum allowable emission)
   [e] none of these

T. Żylicz, *Marketable Permits*, SpringerBriefs in Economics
https://doi.org/10.1007/978-3-032-12133-2

4. The Clean Development Mechanism (CDM)

   [a] **lets non-Annex I countries earn emission reduction 'credits' by undertaking projects that result in GHG emission lower than otherwise expected**
   [b] lets Annex-I countries earn emission reduction credits by undertaking projects that result in GHG emission lower than otherwise expected
   [c] results from the establishment of a cap (upper limit) for global GHG emissions
   [d] results from the establishment of a cap (upper limit) for GHG emissions in Annex I countries
   [e] none of these

5. The 1990 US Clean Air Act amendments authorised environmental protection administrators to

   [a] develop effective policies to combat climate change
   [b] impose energy efficiency standards for buildings
   [c] impose energy efficiency standards for newly manufactured cars
   [d] **launch a country-wide programme to reduce sulphur dioxide emission**
   [e] none of these

6. The ETS

   [a] led to a decrease in the global emission of GHG (greenhouse gases)
   [b] **covers major European plants that emit carbon dioxide**
   [c] is characterised by a constant cap (upper limit of emission)
   [d] was extended in 2024 to accommodate some of non-Annex I countries
   [e] none of these

7. The Chorzów project launched by the Polish Ministry of Environment

   [a] was aimed at forcing major local polluters to comply with European standards
   [b] forced both the steel mill and power plant to abandon their legal actions against the local administrator
   [c] exempted the major local polluters from paying emission charges
   [d] **encouraged the local administrator to enforce stricter requirements with respect to the polluter whose abatement cost was lower**
   [e] none of these

8. California's LCFS programme

   [a] succeeded at eliminating gasoline produced from oil deposits
   [b] requires fuel producers to use domestic (American) raw materials only

[c] **mandates that fuels sold at gas stations imply (on average) decreasing emissions of carbon dioxide**
[d] was found to violate federal legislation
[e] none of these

9. Transferable Development Rights

[a] are the most widespread instrument for biodiversity protection
[b] allow to solve global biodiversity protection problems in a satisfactory way
[c] allow environmental authorities to calculate compensations so that these are paid out easier than when 'standard' instruments are applied
[d] state that in non-protected areas development projects can be carried out without any constraints
[e] **none of these**

Explanations

In every question there is one correct answer (printed in **bold**). However it is always important to identify the reasons why all of the other answers are wrong.

1. The correct answer is [e] *none of these*, as explained in Chap. 2. Here are the reasons why the other ones are wrong. [a] states that *abatement costs should be consistent with accounting regulations*. In most subsidy programmes there is a condition that only certain (specified) cost categories can be repaid (so-called qualified expenditures). This principle is sometimes understood incorrectly as 'cost-effectiveness'. Its correct definition refers to cost minimisation, and not to confirming that the costs actually paid comply with some regulations. [b] and [c]—*the policy is adopted by a democratically elected government* and *the policy is approved in a democratic procedure*—indicate how the policy was arrived at. It is good for an environmental policy to be adopted democratically, but cost-effectiveness does not refer to it. Likewise [d]—*environmental protection is understood in a holistic way (nature cannot be separated into air, water and soil components)*—is something that many environmentalists would be pleased to hear, but it has nothing to do with cost-effectiveness.

2. The correct answer is [b] *allowed higher discharges from paper mills to be compensated by lower discharges from municipal sewage treatment plants (or* vice versa*)*, as explained in Chap. 3. Here are the reasons why the other ones are incorrect. [a] says *allowed agricultural pollution caused by excessive fertiliser application to be compensated by more effective municipal sewage treatment.* No. The experiment allowed one of the 14 sources (a paper mill or a municipal sewage treatment plant) to 'compensate' for another. But it did not take into account the pollution from agricultural land. [c] says *allowed higher current*

discharges to be compensated by lower discharges in the future. No. The experiment did not include any provisions for intertemporal transfers; the river was supposed to be protected every year by the same maximum limit of discharges. [d] says *required discharges from paper mills to be justified by the production sold.* No. This was an absolute level instrument. Unlike some other systems, it did not allow relating permits to any production circumstances.

3. The correct answer is [c] *are organised by environmental protection authorities*, as explained in Chap. 4. Technically the auction can be carried out by a private entity, but it would act on behalf of some public authority. In particular, the authority decides on the quantity of permits to be auctioned. [a] and [b] say, respectively, *provide a good platform for selling emission reduction 'credits'* and *provide an opportunity for firms that undertake abatement projects to sell the results of their emission reduction.* It is possible to sell the outcomes of someone's abatement on secondary markets. At an auction—i.e. on the primary market—firms buy permits to emit. [d] says *provide an opportunity to change the cap (maximum allowable emission).* No. The cap is fixed. Firms that participate in the auction know that it cannot be changed.

4. The correct answer is [a] *lets non-Annex I countries earn emission reduction credits by undertaking projects that result in GHG emission lower than otherwise expected*, as explained in Chap. 5. [b]—*lets Annex-I countries earn emission reduction credits by undertaking projects that result in GHG emission lower than otherwise expected*—is wrong, since CDM is for non-Annex I countries. Also [c] and [d]—*results from the establishment of a cap (upper limit) for global GHG emissions* and *results from the establishment of a cap (upper limit) for GHG emissions in Annex I countries*—are wrong, because non-Annex I countries (which earn CDM 'credits') do not have any caps. If they are given any 'credits', the caps established for Annex I countries become irrelevant.

5. The correct answer is [d] *launch a country-wide programme to reduce sulphur dioxide emission*, as explained in Chap. 6. [a], [b] and [c]—*develop effective policies to combat climate change, impose energy efficiency standards for buildings* and *impose energy efficiency standards for newly manufactured cars*—did not result from the 1990 amendments; American governments addressed these issues later on, but this was not a matter of legislative changes introduced in 1990.

6. The correct answer is [b] *covers major European plants that emit carbon dioxide*, as explained in Chap. 7. The other answers are wrong. [a]—*led to a decrease in the global emission of GHG (greenhouse gases)*—is incorrect since the global emission actually increased dramatically. [c] and [d]—*is characterised by a constant cap (upper limit of emission)* and *was extended in 2024*

to accommodate some of the non-Annex I countries—are incorrect statements as well since European caps decrease over time and the ETS cannot be extended to include non-Annex I countries.

7. The correct answer is [d] *encouraged the local administrator to enforce stricter requirements with respect to the polluter whose abatement cost was lower*, as explained in Chap. 8. [a]—*was aimed at forcing major local polluters to comply with European standards*—is incorrect; please note that Poland acceded the European Union 13 years later. [b]—*forced both the steel mill and power plant to abandon their legal actions against the local administrator*—is wrong too; no legal actions against the local administrator were undertaken. Also the answer [c]—*exempted the major local polluters from paying emission charges*—is wrong because they did have to pay emission charges.

8. The correct answer is [c] *mandates that fuels sold at gas stations imply (on average) decreasing emissions of carbon dioxide*, as explained in Chap. 9. [a] and [b]—*succeeded at eliminating gasoline produced from oil deposits* and *requires fuel producers to use domestic (American) raw materials only*—are wrong. LCFS did not introduce such constraints. Gas stations in California can sell non-American fuels and products originating from geological deposits. [d] *was found to violate federal legislation* is an incorrect statement too; LCFS are consistent with federal legislation.

9. The correct answer is [e] *none of these*, as explained in Chap. 10. [a] and [b]—*are the most widespread instrument for biodiversity protection* and *allow to solve global biodiversity protection problems in a satisfactory way*—are incorrect, because transferable development rights are not widespread, and global biodiversity problems have not been solved. [c] *allow environmental authorities to calculate compensations so that these are paid out easier than when 'standard' instruments are applied* is wrong, since the rationale for transferable development rights is to free authorities from paying compensations. [d] *state that in non-protected areas development projects can be carried out without any constraints* is incorrect as well, since non-protected areas do face some constraints; otherwise there would be no demand for permits supplied by real estate owners in protected areas.

MIX
Papier aus verantwortungsvollen Quellen
Paper from responsible sources
FSC® C105338

If you have any concerns about our products,
you can contact us on
ProductSafety@springernature.com

In case Publisher is established outside the EU,
the EU authorized representative is:
Springer Nature Customer Service Center GmbH
Europaplatz 3, 69115 Heidelberg, Germany

Printed by Libri Plureos GmbH
in Hamburg, Germany